BASIC
BIBLE
PROPHECY

RON RHODES

HARVEST HOUSE PUBLISHERS
EUGENE, OREGON

Cover design by Studio Gearbox

Cover photo © IgorZh, Stavchansky Yakov, ruskpp, ANGHI / Shutterstock; Yoeml / istock

Interior design by Chad Dougherty

For bulk, special sales, or ministry purchases, please call 1-800-547-8979.
Email: Customerservice@hhpbooks.com

Basic Bible Prophecy

Copyright © 2021 by Ron Rhodes
Published by Harvest House Publishers
Eugene, Oregon 97408
www.harvesthousepublishers.com

ISBN 978-0-7369-8033-3 (pbk.)
ISBN 978-0-7369-8034-0 (eBook)

Library of Congress Cataloging-in-Publication Data

Names: Rhodes, Ron, author.
Title: Basic Bible prophecy / Ron Rhodes.
Description: Eugene, Oregon : Harvest House Publishers, [2021] | Includes
    bibliographical references. | Summary: "Primarily for curious newcomers,
    Basic Bible Prophecy is a straightforward breakdown of what you need to
    know about the future. Bestselling prophecy author Ron Rhodes provides a
    big-picture overview of the essential facts about Bible prophecy"–
    Provided by publisher.
Identifiers: LCCN 2020029047 (print) | LCCN 2020029048 (ebook) | ISBN
    9780736980333 (trade paperback) | ISBN 9780736980340 (ebook)
Subjects: LCSH: Bible—Prophecies. | End of the world—Biblical teaching.
Classification: LCC BS647.3 .R426 2021 (print) | LCC BS647.3 (ebook) |
    DDC 220.1/5—dc23
LC record available at https://lccn.loc.gov/2020029047
LC ebook record available at https://lccn.loc.gov/2020029048

Printed in the United States of America

21 22 23 24 25 26 27 28 29 / BP-CD / 10 9 8 7 6 5 4 3 2

*I dedicate this book to the
countless Christians who are new to Bible prophecy,
and who may think it is too complicated to learn.
I promise you—this book makes it easy.
I pray it blesses you!*

Acknowledgments

Through the years, I have received countless letters and emails from people around the world, asking a variety of interesting questions about Bible prophecy. In many cases, people were confused about some aspect of prophecy. In other cases, people voiced concern about the proper chronology of prophetic events. In still other cases, people were intimidated by Bible prophecy, but still expressed interest in trying to learn about it.

I appreciate each of you for taking the time to write. You have motivated me to author this book, which is an introductory guide to the end times. Perhaps for the first time, you will learn all about the WHO, WHAT, WHEN, WHERE, and WHY of Bible prophecy. This book will make it easy.

I want to express my profound thanks to God for the wondrous gift of my family—Kerri, David, and Kylie. Without their endless love and support, the sun would not shine as bright in my world. "I thank my God through Jesus Christ for all of you" (Romans 1:8).

Continued heartfelt appreciation goes to the entire staff at Harvest House Publishers. It has been a pleasure working with this fine publisher through these many years. The professionalism and commitment to truth among the staff are shining examples among Christian publishers. "God...will not forget how hard you have worked for him" (Hebrews 6:10).

Most importantly, I remain ever grateful to the Lord Jesus for the opportunity He has given me to serve Him during this short earthly life.

Come soon, Lord!

CONTENTS

Introduction: Basic Bible Prophecy 7

PART 1: *HOW* CAN WE MAKE SENSE OF BIBLE PROPHECY?
1. How Is Bible Prophecy Important? 15
2. How Can We Understand Last-Days Lingo? 21
3. How Do God's Covenants Relate to Prophecy? 33
4. How Can We Decide on a Literal Versus Allegorical Approach? 41
5. How Can We Properly Interpret Bible Prophecy? 51
6. How Can We Avoid Prophetic Imbalances? 61

PART 2: *WHO* ARE THE PRIMARY PERSONALITIES OF THE END TIMES?
7. Who Are the Bad Guys? 75
8. Who Are the Spiritual Beings Behind the Scenes? 89
9. Who Are the Good Guys? 101

PART 3: *WHAT* ARE THE PRIMARY EVENTS OF THE END TIMES? *WHEN* DO THEY OCCUR?
10. Events Before the Tribulation Period 117
11. Events in the First and Second Halves of the Tribulation 131
12. Events at the End of (and Right After) the Tribulation 143
13. Events in the Millennial Kingdom 153
14. Events Prior to and During the Eternal State 161

PART 4: *WHERE* IN THE WORLD WILL END-TIME PROPHECIES UNFOLD?
15. WHERE in the World: Part 1 173
16. WHERE in the World: Part 2 185

PART 5: *WHY* DOES GOD GIVE US PROPHECIES OF THE END TIMES?
17. A Motivation to Live Expectantly 197
18. A Motivation to Live Righteously 203
19. A Motivation to Live with an Eternal Perspective 211

Postscript: Basic Bible Prophecy Quick Quiz 219
Bibliography 221
Notes 222

Basic Bible Prophecy

Dear reader, if you have ever shied away from studying Bible prophecy because you thought it was too big a topic or perhaps too controversial—with too many conflicting views—*this book is for you.* I take the complicated and make it simple. You may consider this book "Bible prophecy made plain."

It may be that you have studied Bible prophecy before, but you are still confused by it. If that is the case, this book can help dispel your confusion. You will quickly gain clarity and become conversant on all the big issues of prophecy.

I will function as your Bible prophecy tour guide. I will help you understand what you need to know while avoiding unnecessary clutter.

Reading this book will enable you to grasp—perhaps for the first time—both the big picture of Bible prophecy and the most important finer details. The charts and visuals throughout the book will help keep things simple.

In this book I will examine the WHO, WHAT, WHEN, WHERE, and WHY of Bible prophecy. You may think of these categories as different vantage points for studying this important subject.

Different vantage points are a good thing. A police officer who writes up a report on a fender bender will typically interview several witnesses. Each witness has a different vantage point. The officer might interview one person who was walking along the sidewalk when the accident occurred. He might interview another person driving in the car behind the vehicle involved in the accident. He might also interview the person who was looking out the office window at the exact moment the accident occurred. And, of course, he will interview the people involved in the accident. By combining the statements from people with different vantage points, the officer has a much better understanding of what occurred.

The same is true as we study Bible prophecy. By considering the WHO, WHAT, WHEN, WHERE, and WHY we will have a much better understanding of Bible prophecy. I hope you find this to be true as you go through the book.

As a bonus, each chapter will close with some bullet points that summarize the big ideas that you need to remember. I will also include some "questions for reflection" that will help you think through the significance of what you have learned. I think you will find the book to be an enriching experience.

If you are like me, you will soon discover that an understanding of Bible prophecy can be life-changing. My exposure to biblical prophecy was a big contributing factor to my becoming a Christian way back in the 1970s. As a new Christian, I found that the more I studied Bible prophecy, the more I came to understand that—

- God truly knows the future.
- The Bible—which contains God's prophecies of the future—is the Word of God, and you can trust it.
- God is in sovereign control of all that occurs in the world.
- God has a plan for humanity—and He has a plan for you and me.
- God will one day providentially cause good to triumph over evil.
- A new world is coming—a new earth and new heavens, a new city in which to live (the New Jerusalem), and new resurrection bodies that never age, get sick, or die.
- We will experience a joyful reunion with all our Christian loved ones in the afterlife.
- The Lord is coming sooner than we think!

Factors such as these make this book extremely relevant.

Our God Is an Awesome God

One of the most significant benefits growing out of my personal study of Bible prophecy is my ever-growing understanding of the awesomeness of God. I think you will experience this benefit as well.

The God who knows the future is wondrous, majestic, and glorious. He is "the First and the Last; there is no other God" (Isaiah 44:6). The prophet Daniel exulted:

> "Praise the name of God forever and ever,
> for he has all wisdom and power.
> He controls the course of world events;
> he removes kings and sets up other kings.
> He gives wisdom to the wise
> and knowledge to the scholars.
> He reveals deep and mysterious things
> and knows what lies hidden in darkness,
> though he is surrounded by light."
> (Daniel 2:20-22)

Our awesome God is all-knowing. He perceives the past and the future with equal clarity. God's knowledge of all things is from the vantage point of eternity. The past (Isaiah 41:22), present (Hebrews 4:13), and future (Isaiah 46:10) are all encompassed in one ever-present "now" to Him. *He sees all!*

God knows all things, both actual and possible (Matthew 11:20-24). Because He knows all things, there can be no increase or decrease in His knowledge. Psalm 147:5 affirms that "His understanding is beyond comprehension" (see also Psalm 33:13-15; 139:11-12; Proverbs 15:3; Isaiah 40:14; Acts 15:18; Hebrews 4:13; 1 John 3:20). Such verses reveal we can trust God when He communicates prophecies about the future to us. *Never doubt it.*

Scripture also portrays God as being sovereign. He rules the universe, controls all things, and is Lord over all (Ephesians 1). There is nothing that can happen in this universe beyond the reach of His control. All forms of existence are under His absolute dominion. Psalm 66:7 affirms that "by his great power he rules forever." Psalm 93:1 affirms that "the LORD is king!" God Himself asserts, "Everything I plan will come to pass, for I do whatever I wish" (Isaiah 46:10). God assures us, "It will all happen as I have planned. It will be as I have decided" (Isaiah 14:24). Proverbs 16:9 tells us, "We can make our plans, but the LORD determines our steps." Proverbs 19:21 likewise says, "You can make many plans, but the LORD's purpose will prevail."

One of my favorite professors at Dallas Theological Seminary was the late Dr. Robert Lightner—affectionately known as Lightning Bob among his students. In one of his books, he offered this great perspective on God's sovereign oversight of human history:

> When viewed from the perspective of Scripture, history is more than the recording of the events of the past. Rather, what has happened in the past, what is happening now, and what will happen in the future is all evidence of the unfolding of the purposeful plan devised by the personal God of the Bible. All the circumstances of life—past, present, and future—fit into the sovereign plan like pieces of a puzzle.[1]

C.S. Lewis, once a professor at Oxford University, sums it up nicely: "History is a story written by the finger of God." His point was that God controls the nations (Job 12:23; Psalm 22:28; Daniel 4:17); He sets up kings and deposes them (Daniel 2:21); and He does all according to His sovereign plan (Acts 4:27-28). *That means you can trust prophecy!*

Peace in the Heart

My friends, supreme peace in the heart is the natural result of trusting that God is not only all-knowing, He also sovereignly oversees all that happens in the world. No matter what we may encounter—no matter how much we do not understand why certain things happen, and no matter how horrible the newspaper headlines may often seem to be—the knowledge that our sovereign God is in control of human history is like a firm anchor amid life's storms. We can be at peace no matter what the future may hold.

I want you to remember this as we continue through the rest of this book. God does not want us to be fearful about the prophetic future. He wants us to have confidence and peace. When Jesus spoke to His followers about the prophetic future, He added these words: "Don't let your hearts be troubled. Trust in God, and trust also in me" (John 14:1). Remember—our personal relationship with Jesus gives us peace, no matter the external circumstances. Jesus affirmed: "I am leaving you with a gift—peace of mind and heart. And the peace I give is a gift the world cannot give. So don't be troubled or afraid" (John 14:27).

GOD'S PEACE FOR CHRISTIANS	
We can have perfect peace.	Isaiah 26:3
Peace can guard the heart.	Philippians 4:7
Peace can rule the heart.	Colossians 3:15
We have peace in Christ.	John 16:33
Do not be troubled.	John 14:27

My experience has taught me this:

- The more I understand about the prophetic future, the greater is my sense of God's awesomeness, power, and might.

- The more I understand of God's awesomeness, power, and might, the greater is the peace in my heart.

May it be the same for you!

HOW CAN WE MAKE SENSE OF BIBLE PROPHECY?

How Is Bible Prophecy Important?

My primary focus in this book is on the WHO, WHAT, WHEN, WHERE, and WHY of Bible prophecy. First, however, I wish to consider HOW we can make sense of Bible prophecy. Toward that end, I want to address some specific questions:

- How is Bible prophecy important?
- How can we understand last-days lingo?
- How do God's covenants relate to prophecy?
- How can we decide between a literal or allegorical approach?
- How can we properly interpret prophecy?
- How can we avoid prophetic imbalances?

After we understand the HOW of Bible prophecy, the other broad categories—the WHO, WHAT, WHEN, WHERE, and WHY—will make much better sense. Trust me. I've been studying prophecy for decades.

We begin with the foundational question: *How is Bible prophecy important?* Studying Bible prophecy is important because it brings some great benefits. These benefits are part of the motivation for studying prophecy. You do not want to miss out on these benefits. Following are seven that are especially meaningful to me.

1. Prophecy Proves God Is the *True* God

The Bible reveals that one proof of the true God—in the face of many false gods and idols—is that He can predict the future. In Isaiah 41:21-23, God challenges people to supply proof that their worthless idols are really gods:

> "Present the case for your idols," says the LORD. "Let them show what they can do," says the King of Israel. "Let them try to tell us what happened long ago so that we may consider the evidence. Or let them tell us what the future holds, so we can know what's going to happen. Yes, tell us what will occur in the days ahead."

These idols and false gods could not comply. By contrast, the true God says of Himself: "Everything I prophesied has come true, and now I will prophesy again. I will tell you the future before it happens" (Isaiah 42:9). He later likewise affirmed: "I alone am God! I am God, and there is none like me. Only I can tell you the future before it even happens. Everything I plan will come to pass, for I do whatever I wish" (Isaiah 46:9-10).

2. Prophecy Proves the Bible Is God's Word

Fulfilled prophecy shows that the Bible is, in fact, the Word of God and can be trusted. The logic is simple:

1. God alone knows the prophetic future.

2. God shares multiple specific prophecies of the future in the pages of the Bible and no other holy book.

3. Over one hundred Old Testament messianic prophecies of Christ's first coming—the fulfillment of each one recorded in the pages of the New Testament—confirm God's 100 percent accuracy rate in foretelling the future.

4. Prophecy is thus a compelling proof that the Bible is God's Word and can be trusted.

3. Prophecy Promotes Evangelism

Prophecy can be a powerful evangelistic tool. We find a perfect example of this in Peter's sermon delivered on the day of Pentecost, after all kinds of supernatural phenomena had just occurred. Peter began his message by speaking about prophecy related to the outpouring of the Holy Spirit upon people: "What you see was predicted long ago by the prophet Joel" (Acts 2:16). Later in the sermon, Peter moved into his evangelistic pitch: "Everyone who calls on the name of the LORD will be saved" (2:21). The result? "Those who believed what Peter said were baptized and added to the church that day—about 3,000 in all" (2:41).

I can personally confirm the powerful effect of Bible prophecy as a tool of evangelism. In my teens, I was a member of a liberal Christian church. I had never trusted in Christ for salvation. Everything changed once I started to study Bible prophecy. Prophecy got my attention! I not only became a true believer in Jesus, but I became insatiably hungry for God's Word. The study of prophecy was a significant turning point in my life.

4. Prophecy Comforts Us in Our Grief

Prophecy can have a profoundly positive effect on us when we lose a Christian loved one in death. The Thessalonian Christians had lost some of their loved ones and asked the apostle Paul whether they would experience the rapture, that glorious future event in which the dead in Christ will be resurrected and living Christians will be instantly translated into their resurrection bodies—and both groups will be caught up to meet Christ in the air and taken back to heaven (John 14:1-3; 1 Corinthians 15:51-54; 1 Thessalonians 4:13-17).

Since these Christians were so concerned about the matter, Paul provided them a full explanation:

> Dear brothers and sisters, we want you to know what will happen to the believers who have died so you will not grieve like people who have no hope. For since we believe that Jesus died and was raised to life again, we also believe that when Jesus returns, God will bring back with him the believers who have died.

> We tell you this directly from the Lord: We who are still living when the Lord returns will not meet him ahead of those who have died. For the Lord himself will come down from heaven with a commanding shout, with the voice of the archangel, and with the trumpet call of God. First, the believers who have died will rise from their graves. Then, together with them, we who are still alive and remain on the earth will be caught up in the clouds to meet the Lord in the air. Then we will be with the Lord forever. So encourage each other with these words (1 Thessalonians 4:13-18).

Of course, it is natural for us to still experience grief when a Christian loved one dies. But we will not grieve "like people who have no hope." We know that a reunion is coming. We will be with our Christian loved ones again. Someone said, "No two Christians will ever meet for the last time." I think that is true.

5. Prophecy Can Strengthen Believers Facing Adversity

The original recipients of the prophetic book of Revelation were Christians who lived about sixty-five years after Jesus experienced crucifixion and then was raised from the dead. Many of these were second-generation Christians, and the challenges they faced were enormous. Their lives had become increasingly difficult because of Roman hostilities against Christianity.

The recipients of the book were suffering from persecution, and some of them were even being martyred (Revelation 2:13). Unfortunately, things were about to get even worse. The book of Revelation was intended to give these believers a strong sense of hope that would help them patiently endure amid relentless suffering. *Human suffering is temporal, but our eternal life with God is forever.* As my old friend Walter Martin used to put it, "I read the last chapter in the book, and we win!" We need to keep this in mind whenever we face adversity.

6. Prophecy Proves God Will Triumph Over Evil

Part of the "big win" for believers is that in the afterlife, the antichrist, the false prophet, and Satan will experience eternal quarantine in the lake of fire (Revelation 19:20; 20:10). Meanwhile, resurrected believers—no longer having a sin nature—will live directly in God's presence in the New Jerusalem, the eternal city of the redeemed:

> "Look, God's home is now among his people! He will live with them, and they will be his people. God himself will be with them. He will wipe every tear from their eyes, and there will be no more death or sorrow or crying or pain. All these things are gone forever." And the one sitting on the throne said, "Look, I am making everything new!" (Revelation 21:3-5).

Evil will be gone forever!

7. Prophecy Brings Special Blessings

Right at the beginning of the book of Revelation, we are told: "God blesses the one who reads the words of this prophecy to the church, and he blesses all who listen to its message and obey what it says, for the time is near" (Revelation 1:3). This is the first of seven pronouncements of special blessing in the book of Revelation (see 14:13; 16:15; 19:9; 20:6; 22:7,14). You will notice from these verses that *obedience brings the blessing*. We should not be just *hearers* of God's prophetic Word, but *doers* of it (James 1:22-25).

My friends, I share all this so you won't consider the study of prophecy just an academic exercise. It not only informs the brain, but it also deeply touches the heart. Our lives can change for the better because of studying Bible prophecy. Don't miss out!

The Big Ideas

- Prophecy proves God is the *true* God.
- Prophecy proves the Bible is God's Word and can be trusted.
- Prophecy promotes evangelism.
- Prophecy comforts us in our grief.

- Prophecy can strengthen believers facing adversity.
- Prophecy proves God will triumph over evil.
- Prophecy can bring special blessings.

Questions for Reflection

1. What are three of the most meaningful things you learned about prophecy in this chapter?
2. What changes might you want to make in your life in view of what you have learned about prophecy so far?

How Can We Understand
Last-Days Lingo?

When I first became a Christian as a teenager, I had a discussion with a friend about Bible prophecy. We knew next to nothing about the subject. We were newbies, wet behind the ears in every way. We had *no idea* what we were talking about.

At that time, all we had was a King James Bible. So we opened it one day and read a prophecy in Luke 21:11 that affirmed: "Great earthquakes shall be in divers places." At first, we thought there might be underwater earthquakes—where *divers* go. And then it suddenly dawned on us: "Oh, wait a minute. This must be an Old English way of referring to 'diverse places,' as in *different places.*"

All these years later, having taught many Christians about Bible prophecy, I can tell you that it is easy to get confused over prophecy lingo. Terms like *eschatology* and *apocalyptic* can seem like a foreign language to some people. We might call that foreign language *Christianese.*

If you are new to Bible prophecy, some of these Christianese terms may be unfamiliar to you. That is okay. No problem. I authored this book to make things simple. I will explain it all. You will soon be conversant in basic Bible prophecy! And you will be able to impress your friends with big words like *eschatology* and *apocalyptic.*

UNDERSTANDING PROPHETS

The word *prophet* comes from the Hebrew word *nabi.* You do not need to remember that. The thing you *do* need to remember is that a prophet is a *spokesman for God*. And that spokesman typically had two roles in Bible times:

1. Sometimes God's prophets directed their words at specific contemporary situations or problems that needed attention back in Bible times. (Their message might be as simple as "stop sinning," or "turn back to God.")

2. At other times, God's prophets foretold the future based on divine revelation (see 2 Samuel 7:27; Jeremiah 23:18).

In both cases, the prophets typically prefaced their words with, "Thus saith the Lord." Their words were not their own but came from God. The divine source of their words gave their words authority.

There are cases in the Old Testament where God's human messenger spoke forth a prophetic word, and in the New Testament we are told that *God is the one who said it*. This proves that God was the ultimate source of their prophetic words.

GOD SPEAKS THROUGH THE PROPHETS	
Old Testament Reference	New Testament Reference
Psalmist said (Psalm 95:7)	Holy Spirit said (Hebrews 3:7)
Psalmist said (Psalm 45:6)	God said (Hebrews 1:8)
Psalmist said (Psalm 102:25,27)	God said (Hebrews 1:10-12)
Isaiah said (Isaiah 7:14)	The Lord spoke by the prophet (Matthew 1:22-23)
Hosea said (Hosea 11:1)	The Lord spoke by the prophet (Matthew 2:15)
Eliphaz's words (Job 5:13)	God's Word (1 Corinthians 3:19)

These men did not just wake up one day and say, "I want to be a prophet." Rather, God Himself called the prophets into service (Jeremiah 1:5; Luke 1:13-16). These prophets came from all walks of life—from farmers (Amos 7:14) to princes (Genesis 23:6). Whatever their background, the prophets were messengers of the Lord (Isaiah 44:26) who served God and shepherded God's people (Amos 3:7; Zechariah 11:4,7; Jeremiah 17:16).

Messages of Judgment or Comfort

Some prophets carried out their work *before* Israel went into captivity. Captivity involved bondage to another more-powerful country as a form of God's disciplinary judgment on Israel. Because of Israel's sin and complacency, these prophets warned that a time of judgment was coming. God would not allow the sins of His people to continue (see, for example, Amos 9:1-10). Though the prophets called the people to repentance, the people became hardened in their sin, and disciplinary judgment therefore inevitably came. They went into captivity. (An example is the Jewish captivity in Babylon—Daniel 1.)

When the people of Israel perceived that God had allowed their bondage because of their sins, they became despondent as they realized they had ultimately brought this on themselves. The prophets therefore spoke soothing words of comfort, promising that God still had a plan for their future and would one day deliver them from their suffering (Isaiah 6:13; 28:5; 29:5; 31:5).

Different Styles

Prophets received messages from God in various ways, including visions, dreams, and even hearing God's voice. Likewise, the prophets used multiple means in delivering their messages. Sometimes they might deliver a simple proclamation in a sanctuary. At other times they might speak face-to-face with an individual. And at other times they might act out their message (see Jeremiah 19). Isaiah even went barefoot and naked for three years in pointing to the embarrassing shame of his people (Isaiah 20:2-3). (Yes, I know, that is bizarre.) Regardless of the means the prophets used in delivering their messages, God expected the people to hear and obey.

Major and Minor Prophets

There are two categories of prophets: The major prophets were

Isaiah, Jeremiah, Ezekiel, and Daniel. These guys were the "big wheels." The minor prophets were Hosea, Joel, Amos, Obadiah, Jonah, Micah, Nahum, Habakkuk, Zephaniah, Haggai, Zechariah, and Malachi. These guys were the "small fries." Nevertheless, their words were just as much from God as the divine words the major prophets received. God spoke through *all* of them.

The Prophets Never Made Mistakes When Speaking for God

Some people claim the prophet Jonah made a mistake when he prophesied that God would overthrow Nineveh in forty days. Jonah's prediction did not come to pass.

Jonah did not make a mistake, however, for he told the Ninevites precisely what God told him to say (see Jonah 3:1-2). There was apparently a repentance clause built into Jonah's prophecy. The Ninevites understood that God would overthrow Nineveh in forty days *unless they repented* (Jonah 3:5-9). Based on how the Ninevites responded in repentance to Jonah's prophecy, God withdrew the threatened punishment.

Let me clue you in to an important Bible passage. In Jeremiah 18:7-8, God Himself affirmed: "If I announce that a certain nation or kingdom is to be uprooted, torn down, and destroyed, but then that nation renounces its evil ways, I will not destroy it as I had planned." This is the "repentance clause" I was talking about.

Nineveh renounced its evil, and God responded with mercy (see Exodus 32:14; 2 Samuel 24:16; Amos 7:3,6). God always loves to show mercy where repentance is evident.

The biblical prophets were always 100 percent accurate. If a prophet was less than 100 percent accurate, the people stoned him to death as a false prophet (Deuteronomy 13; 18:20-22).

GOD'S PROPHETS		
Jonah	781 BC	Prophesied to Nineveh
Amos	765–754 BC	Prophesied to Israel
Isaiah	760–673 BC	Prophesied to Judah
Hosea	758–725 BC	Prophesied to Israel
Micah	738–698 BC	Prophesied to Judah
Nahum	658–615 BC	Prophesied about Nineveh
Jeremiah	650–582 BC	Prophesied to Judah
Zephaniah	640–626 BC	Prophesied to Judah
Ezekiel	620–570 BC	Prophesied in Babylon
Daniel	620–540 BC	Prophesied in Babylon
Habakkuk	608–598 BC	Prophesied to Judah
Obadiah	590 BC	Prophesied about Edom
Zechariah	522–509 BC	Prophesied to Judah
Haggai	520 BC	Prophesied to Judah
Malachi	465 BC	Prophesied to Judah
Joel	450 BC	Prophesied to Judah

Prophecy

Now that we know what a prophet is, allow me to add just a few words about prophecy—especially predictive prophecy of the future. Some Bible experts define prophecy in modern vernacular as "history written in advance." I think it is more precise to say that prophecy is God's revelation regarding history in advance, for only God in His omniscience—His *all-knowingness*—knows the future. God makes this claim in Isaiah 46:9-11:

> "Remember the things I have done in the past.
>   For I alone am God!
>   I am God, and there is none like me.
> Only I can tell you the future

before it even happens.
Everything I plan will come to pass,
    for I do whatever I wish...
I have said what I would do,
    and I will do it."

The word *prophesy* (as opposed to *prophecy*) means to set forth prophecies. Everything God prophesies eventually comes to pass. You can count on it. God makes this claim in Isaiah 48:3:

"Long ago I told you what was going to happen.
    Then suddenly I took action,
    and all my predictions came true."

He likewise affirms in Isaiah 42:8-9:

"I am the Lord; that is my name!
    I will not give my glory to anyone else,
    nor share my praise with carved idols.
Everything I prophesied has come true,
    and now I will prophesy again.
I will tell you the future before it happens."

These verses reveal that our sovereign God controls human history. What He predicts (or *prophesies*) always comes to pass. He is the only one who can show the future to us. And He does this through prophecies recorded in the pages of the Bible.

A Case Study: Fulfilled Prophecies of the Past

Many of the prophecies God set forth in Old Testament times find fulfillment in New Testament times. For example, over one hundred messianic prophecies find a literal fulfillment in the first coming of Jesus back in the first century. That is a lot!

Jesus often showed His listeners He was the specific fulfillment of Old Testament messianic prophecy. He made the following comments to people on different occasions:

- "This is all happening to fulfill the words of the prophets as recorded in the Scriptures" (Matthew 26:56).

- "Jesus took them through the writings of Moses and all the prophets, explaining from all the Scriptures the things concerning himself" (Luke 24:27).

- "When I was with you before, I told you that everything written about me in the law of Moses and the prophets and in the Psalms must be fulfilled" (Luke 24:44).

- Jesus told some Jewish critics: "You search the Scriptures because you think they give you eternal life. But the Scriptures point to me!" (John 5:39-40).

- Jesus also said to some Jewish critics: "If you really believed Moses, you would believe me, because he wrote about me" (John 5:46-47).

- We read of Jesus in a synagogue: "He rolled up the scroll, handed it back to the attendant, and sat down. All eyes in the synagogue looked at him intently. Then he began to speak to them. 'The Scripture you've just heard has been fulfilled this very day!'" (Luke 4:20-21).

Among the literally fulfilled prophecies are that the Messiah would be born of a virgin (Isaiah 7:14), from the line of Abraham (Genesis 12:2-3), from the line of David (2 Samuel 7:12-16), in the city of Bethlehem (Micah 5:2), suffer betrayal for thirty shekels of silver (Zechariah 11:12), suffer crucifixion for our sins (Zechariah 12:10) while dying with criminals (Isaiah 53:12), and experience resurrection from the dead (Psalm 16:10). Jesus fulfilled these and many more messianic prophecies in the Old Testament.

Such fulfilled prophecies give us strong confidence to expect that prophecies of our future will find just as literal a fulfillment. God's fulfillment of past prophecies establishes an unbroken pattern of literal fulfillment. He has set a precedent. This leads me to a principle that you should never forget:

> **If you want to understand how God will fulfill prophecy in the future, just take a look at how He has fulfilled prophecy in the past.**

What in the World Is Eschatology?

Eschatology is a big fancy word used by theologians who teach in seminaries. It derives from two Greek words—*eschatos*, meaning "last" or "last things," and *logos*, meaning "study of." Eschatology is the study of last things. It is the study of the end times. It is the study of prophecy. It is pronounced *es-kuh-TOL-uh-jee*. Easy enough, right?

I believe the study of eschatology is essential. I say this because 25 percent of Scripture was prophetic when first written. Many of these end-time Bible verses address the rapture, the tribulation period, the antichrist, the false prophet, Armageddon, the second coming of Christ, and heaven and the afterlife. (I will fully explain all these terms later in the book.)

There are two categories of eschatology: *Personal eschatology* concerns such things as death, the future judgment, heaven, and hell. These are matters that relate to each person. *General eschatology* concerns more general prophetic issues, such as the rapture, the tribulation period, and the second coming. Both categories of eschatology are important.

What in the World Is Apocalyptic Literature?

Apocalyptic is another one of those big words theologians like to use in seminaries. But it is actually easy to understand. The Greek word for apocalypse means "revelation" or "unveiling." Apocalyptic literature contains divine revelations that unveil the future. The word is pronounced *uh-paa-kuh-LIP-tuk*.

Apocalyptic literature arose among the Jews and Christians in Bible times to reveal certain mysteries about heaven and earth, especially about the world to come. Such literature features visions, the necessity of making ethical and moral decisions or changes because of these visions, and a pervasive use of symbols.

Seven primary themes are common to apocalyptic literature:

1. A growing sense of hopelessness as wicked powers grow in strength

2. The promise that God will intervene

3. Heavenly visions that provide readers with a divine perspective that helps them endure present suffering

4. The intervention of God in overcoming and destroying evil

5. The call to believers to live righteously

6. The call to believers to persevere under trial

7. God's final deliverance and restoration, with the promise to dwell with His people forever

The book of Revelation is an excellent example of apocalyptic literature. It contains heavenly visions and provides hope, inspiration, and comfort to persecuted believers. It shows that God will ultimately win over evil and that Christians will one day live face-to-face with Him in the afterlife.

Another well-known apocalyptic book is Daniel. It has many prophecies of the end times. It tells us a lot about the tribulation period and the rise of the antichrist (Daniel 2; 7; 9:26-27). It is helpful to study the books of Revelation and Daniel side by side, in concert with each other. They complement each other rather well.

The Last Days

Several New Testament passages use "last days," "last times," and "last time" to refer to the present church age in which we now live. For example, the writer of Hebrews said, "Long ago, at many times and in many ways, God spoke to our fathers by the prophets, but in these last days he has spoken to us by his Son" (Hebrews 1:1-2 ESV). We also read of Christ in 1 Peter 1:20: "God chose him as your ransom long before the world began, but now in these last days he has been revealed for your sake." These verses show that people in New Testament times up to the present day are, in some sense, already in the "last days."

The term has a different meaning in the Old Testament. Indeed, when the Old Testament uses the term, it prophetically refers to Israel in the seven-year tribulation period, after which the divine Messiah comes again and sets up His millennial kingdom on earth (see, for example, Deuteronomy 4:30).

As we study biblical prophecy, it is wise to keep in mind how the Old and New Testaments use these terms differently. This distinction helps us to be interpreters who are "accurately handling the word of truth" (2 Timothy 2:15 NASB).

The End Times

The term *end times* is a broad phrase that embraces many events that transpire during the prophesied last days. These include the rapture, the judgment seat of Christ (for Christians), the tribulation period, Armageddon, the second coming of Christ, the millennial kingdom, and the great white throne judgment (for the wicked). Also included are heaven (for believers) and hell (for unbelievers). All these are part and parcel of the end times.

Other Terms

There are all kinds of other Christianese terms used in the study of Bible prophecy—and they're not for the faint of heart. Here are three terms that describe the three primary views Christians have on the timing of the rapture:

- *Pretribulationism* holds that the rapture will occur *before* the tribulation period.

- *Midtribulationism* says the rapture will occur at the *midpoint* of the tribulation.

- *Posttribulationism* says the rapture will occur *after* the tribulation period.

There are also three terms that describe the three primary views Christians have on Christ's future millennial kingdom:

- *Amillennialism* (literally "*no* millennium") holds that there is no literal future millennial kingdom, but rather Christ simply reigns over the church from heaven.

- *Postmillennialism* (literally "*after* the millennium") holds that Christ's second coming will occur after an extended time—metaphorically described as a thousand years— during which the church will Christianize the entire world.

- *Premillennialism* (literally "*before* the millennium") holds that Christ will come again prior to a literal millennial kingdom, which will feature a one-thousand-year rule of Christ on earth.

Phew! Take a deep breath and repeat after me: "I don't have to remember all these terms just yet." But here's a spoiler alert: I believe in *pretribulationism* and *premillennialism*. (I'll tell you why later in the book.)

The Big Ideas

- Prophets are God's spokesmen who often reveal the future based on divine revelation.

- Prophecy is God's revelation of history written in advance.

- Already-fulfilled prophecies give us strong confidence to expect that prophecies of our future will find just as literal a fulfillment as the earlier ones.

- Eschatology is a fancy term referring to a study of prophecy.

- The Bible contains two apocalyptic books: Revelation and Daniel, both of which "unveil" the future by divine revelations. It is helpful to study these side by side.

- The term *last days* in the Old Testament refers to Israel in the seven-year tribulation period.

- *End times* is a general term embracing many events that transpire during the prophesied last days.

Questions for Reflection

1. How important do you think prophecy is to God, given that 25 percent of the Bible was prophetic when originally written? How important should prophecy be to you?

2. Do you ever find yourself pondering the afterlife (personal eschatology)? What thoughts come to your mind? Do these thoughts motivate righteous behavior?

3

How Do God's Covenants Relate to Prophecy?

A covenant is simply an agreement between two parties. In Bible times, various nations made covenants in the form of treaties or alliances (1 Samuel 11:1). Individual people also formed covenants with each other (Genesis 21:27). Sometimes covenants functioned as friendship pacts (1 Samuel 18:3-4). Every once in a while, someone might make a covenant with himself, as did Job: "I made a covenant with my eyes not to look with lust at a young woman." God, too, formed covenants with His people (Exodus 19:5-6). Covenants were quite common in Bible times.

As we scan through the pages of Scripture, we find that God made covenant promises to many people, including Noah (Genesis 9:8-17), Abraham (Genesis 15:12-21; 17:1-14), the Israelites at Mount Sinai (Exodus 19:5-6), David (2 Samuel 7:13; 23:5), and God's people in the new covenant (Hebrews 8:6-13). *God is a God of promises.*

There were actually two kinds of covenants in Bible times: *conditional* and *unconditional.* A conditional covenant is a covenant with an "if" attached. A conditional covenant between God and human beings, for example, required that human beings meet certain obligations or conditions before God had to fulfill what He promised. If God's people did not meet the requirements, God was not obligated to fulfill His promises.

An unconditional covenant, by contrast, did not depend on such conditions for its fulfillment. There were no *ifs* attached. An unconditional covenant between God and human beings involved God's firm and inviolable promises apart from any merit (or lack thereof) of the human beings to whom God made the promises.

Some Christians prefer the term *unilateral covenant* instead of *unconditional covenant*. The term *unilateral* refers to an action or decision performed by only one person (in this case, God) with no conditions imposed on the other party of the covenant (for example, Israel). Other Christians prefer the designation *one-sided covenant* or *divine commitment covenant*.

CONDITIONAL COVENANT	UNCONDITIONAL COVENANT
Two-sided covenant	One-sided covenant
Entails human and divine commitment	Entails divine commitment alone
Conditions attached	No conditions attached
Blessing hinges on human merit	God blesses regardless of merit
Blessings are earned	Blessings are freely given

Three of the most important covenants in the Bible between God and human beings are the Abrahamic covenant, the Davidic covenant, and the new covenant. The Abrahamic and Davidic covenants have special relevance for the prophetic future of Israel (though Gentiles end up getting blessed as well). The new covenant has both present and future prophetic relevance for all believers—both Jew and Gentile. Let's consider a few specifics.

The Abrahamic Covenant

A famous covenant in the Bible is God's covenant with Abraham (Genesis 12:1-3; 15:18-21). This covenant is so important that God later reaffirmed it with Abraham's son Isaac (17:21; 26:2-5). He also reiterated the covenant with Isaac's son Jacob (28:10-17; 35:10-12). The Bible categorizes this covenant as an *everlasting* covenant (Genesis 17:7-8; 1 Chronicles 16:17; Psalm 105:7-11; Isaiah 24:5).

Before God's enactment of this covenant, He had focused broadly on humankind. God now narrowed the focus to Abraham and his descendants. This represents the beginning of the Jewish people, from whom the Messiah would one day be born (Luke 3:34).

In this covenant, God made seven prophetic promises to Abraham, as recorded in Genesis 12:

1. I will make you a great nation (12:2). This was a remarkable promise from Abraham's perspective. He and Sarah had not yet had a son. And they were in old age. That the Jewish nation would emerge from him and his wife seemed unlikely. With God, however, all things are possible (Mark 10:27).

2. I will bless you (12:2). God's blessing of Abraham involved great wealth (13:2) and substantial material goods (24:35). God favored Abraham (21:22).

3. I will make your name great (12:2). God made Abraham famous, making his name great. Both the Old and New Testaments testify to this. Abraham's reputation was that of an "honored prince" (23:6), "the friend of God" (James 2:23), and "the founder" of "the Jewish nation" (Romans 4:1). Today Abraham is known worldwide by Jews, Christians, and others.

4. I will bless those who bless you (12:3). Charles Ryrie notes: "Abraham's relation to God was so close that to bless or curse him was, in effect, to bless or curse God." So, friends of the Jews are friends of God and experience His blessing.[2]

5. I will curse those who curse you (12:3). Anti-Semites are ultimately anti-God and will experience God's curse.

6. All peoples on earth will experience blessing through you (12:3). This blessing came to fruition when Abraham's descendant, Jesus Christ, was born as the Savior of humankind (Galatians 3:8,16).

7. I will give you and your descendants the land of Canaan (12:1; 15:18-21). This is "the Promised Land" (Psalm 47:4).

God's covenant promises to Abraham were unconditional. This means God made firm and inviolable promises to Abraham that did

not depend on any merit (or lack thereof) on Abraham's part. There
were no *ifs* attached.

We know this to be the case from the way God enacted the covenant with Abraham. According to ancient custom, the two parties of
a conditional covenant would divide an animal into two equal parts
and then walk between the two parts, showing that each was responsi-
ble for fulfilling the obligations of the covenant (see Jeremiah 34:18-19).
With the Abrahamic covenant, however, God alone passed between
the parts after God put Abraham into a deep sleep (Genesis 15:12,17).
This shows that God made unconditional promises to Abraham in this
covenant. Abraham had no obligations to fulfill in order to receive the
covenant promises.

These promises will find their ultimate fulfillment in Christ's
thousand-year millennial kingdom, following the second coming. It
is at that time that Israel will experience total fulfillment of the land
promises given to Abraham. (I will explain the millennial kingdom
later in the book. For now, just remember that it follows the second
coming of Christ.)

The Davidic Covenant

Another famous covenant in the Bible is God's covenant with
David. God in this covenant promised that one of David's descendants would rule forever (2 Samuel 7:12-13; 22:51). Like the Abrahamic covenant, the Davidic covenant is an unconditional covenant. It
did not depend on David in any way for its fulfillment. David realized
this when he received God's promises in the covenant. He appropri-
ately responded with an attitude of humility and a recognition of God's
sovereignty over the affairs of human beings.

The covenant features three notable words: *throne, house,* and *kingdom.* Such words point to the political future of Israel. Israel will be a
royal dynasty. This covenant finds its ultimate fulfillment in the royal
person of Jesus Christ (the royal King of kings), who was born from
the line of David (Matthew 1:1). Christ will one day rule as King on the
throne of David in Jerusalem during the millennial kingdom (Ezekiel
36:1-12; Micah 4:1-5; Zephaniah 3:14-20; Zechariah 14:1-21).

Prior to Jesus's birth in Bethlehem, the angel Gabriel appeared to Mary and informed her, "The Lord God will give to him the throne of his father David, and he will reign over the house of Jacob forever, and of his kingdom there will be no end" (Luke 1:32-33 ESV). Notice the three significant words in this passage—*throne, house,* and *kingdom.* Gabriel's words must have immediately brought these Old Testament promises to mind for Mary, a devout young Jew. Gabriel's words were a clear announcement that the babe in her womb would fulfill the Davidic covenant. Her baby would one day rule on the throne of David in the future kingdom. Gabriel's words were full of prophetic anticipation.

The New Covenant

The new covenant is yet another famous unconditional covenant God made with humankind. In it, God promised to provide for the forgiveness of sin, based entirely on the sacrificial death and resurrection of Jesus Christ (Jeremiah 31:31-34). Under the old covenant, worshippers never enjoyed a sense of total forgiveness. Under the new covenant, however, Christ our High Priest made provisions for such forgiveness.

When Jesus ate the Passover meal with His disciples in the upper room, He spoke of "the new covenant between God and his people—an agreement confirmed with my blood, which is poured out as a sacrifice for you" (Luke 22:20). Jesus did everything necessary for our forgiveness by His once and for all sacrifice on the cross. "God made Christ, who never sinned, to be the offering for our sin, so that we could be made right with God through Christ" (2 Corinthians 5:21).

The new covenant is the basis for our relationship with God in the New Testament. It is a game-changer in our relationship with God. Without these wonderful promises in the new covenant, you and I would have no hope for a future in heaven following death.

Never Forget—God Is a Promise Keeper

Numbers 23:19 asserts, "God is not a man, so he does not lie. He is not human, so he does not change his mind. Has he ever spoken and failed to act? Has he ever promised and not carried it through?" Deuteronomy 7:9 likewise affirms, "The LORD your God is indeed God. He is the faithful God who keeps his covenant for a thousand generations."

An aged Joshua declared, "Not a single one of all the good promises the LORD had given to the family of Israel was left unfulfilled; everything he had spoken came true" (Joshua 21:45). He later affirmed: "Soon I will die, going the way of everything on earth. Deep in your hearts you know that every promise of the LORD your God has come true. Not a single one has failed" (23:14).

Solomon later likewise proclaimed, "Praise the LORD who has given rest to his people Israel, just as he promised. Not one word has failed of all the wonderful promises he gave through his servant Moses" (1 Kings 8:56).

My friends, God truly is faithful. He will fulfill all of His covenant promises. These covenant promises are foundational to the prophetic future. We will see this illustrated in the chapters to come.

We have good reason to rejoice in God's faithfulness!

The Big Ideas

- A covenant is an agreement between two parties.
- The land promise to Israel in the unconditional Abrahamic covenant will be fulfilled in Christ's millennial kingdom, which follows His second coming.
- The throne promise in the unconditional Davidic covenant will be fulfilled when Christ rules on David's throne in the millennial kingdom.
- Our forgiveness of sins is based entirely on the new covenant.
- God is a promise-keeper.

Questions for Reflection

1. What have you learned in this chapter that strengthens

your faith in God? Do you have a strong hope for the future?

2. How does it make you feel to know that the new covenant applies directly to you?

4

How Can We Decide on a Literal Versus Allegorical Approach?

I once encountered a person who took a bizarre allegorical approach to Scripture. I was at a large conference, and this person came up to me out of the blue and commented that Jesus taught Yoga.

"Excuse me?" I said.

"I believe that Jesus taught Yoga," he said.

"What makes you think that?" I asked.

"It's in Matthew 11:29-30, where Jesus said: 'Take my yoke upon you. Let me teach you, because I am humble and gentle at heart, and you will find rest for your souls. For my yoke is easy to bear, and the burden I give you is light.'"

"Hmm, this says 'yoke,' not 'Yoga.'"

He replied that "yoke" and "Yoga" come from the same root word, *yo*, and that Jesus was allegorically teaching Yoga. He affirmed that Yoga is "easy" to learn and can bring "rest" to our souls.

I tried to reason with him. But he remained committed to his allegorical Scripture-twisting.

On another occasion, I came across a liberal Christian who took an allegorical approach to Bible prophecy. I asked him his view on the second coming of Christ. He immediately replied that the second coming occurs whenever a person finds God again within his or her heart. It is not limited to happening just once. It can happen over and over again in the same person's life. He told me that such prophecies were never intended to be taken literally.

Should we interpret Bible prophecy allegorically? Or should we take it literally? Christians love to debate this question!

I must tell you that one's decision in this matter will affect one's entire prophetic outlook. It therefore makes good sense to give serious consideration to it.

Spoiler alert: *I take prophecy literally.* I will tell you why a bit later in the chapter.

Understanding the Allegorical Approach

Let's time-travel back to the early centuries after the time of Christ. Early in the history of the Christian church—right around AD 190, over 150 years after the time of Christ—an allegorical school of interpretation arose in Alexandria, Egypt. This school consistently interpreted Scripture in a nonliteral sense. Proponents of this school sought symbolic meanings in the pages of Scripture.

The allegorical approach became super-popular at this time. The literal approach faded into the background.

The influence of this early emergence of the allegorical method was enormous in subsequent generations. The great theologian Augustine interpreted all of Scripture—except prophecy—in a natural and literal sense. He was inconsistent, however, in interpreting prophecy. He accepted a literal second coming of Christ. He also held to a literal heaven and hell. But he concluded that the millennial kingdom (the thousand-year reign of Christ on earth) *is not* literal. Using an allegorical approach, he suggested that the church was already living in the millennium as part of the spiritual kingdom of God. He said Christ is even now reigning in the hearts of Christians. He denied there would ever be a literal kingdom on earth where Christ would rule.

Augustine's view became the dominant view of the Roman Catholic Church. Reformation luminaries such as Martin Luther and John Calvin also adopted his view. Because such well-known theologians in church history accepted the allegorical method in interpreting prophecies relating to the millennial kingdom, many today have taken the same view. Some today apply the allegorical method not just to the millennium but to other aspects of biblical prophecy.

Here is an important point to remember: Whether one interprets prophecy allegorically or literally will affect how one answers many questions related to biblical prophecy. For example:

- Will the millennial kingdom involve a literal thousand-year reign of Jesus on earth, or does it refer to Christ's present spiritual reign from heaven over the church?

- Do the covenant promises made to Israel in Old Testament times (the Abrahamic and Davidic covenants) relate to Israel, or are they spiritually fulfilled in some way in the church?

- How do we interpret the various judgments in Scripture—the judgment seat of Christ for Christians, the judgment of the nations following Christ's return, and the great white throne judgment of the wicked dead following the millennium? Are they separate and distinct judgments, as literalism holds? Or do they describe one general judgment at the end of the age, as the allegorical school holds?

One's choice in interpretive method is of enormous importance. One should therefore weigh this debate carefully. In what follows, I will present the case for a literal interpretation of prophecy, which I believe to be the correct view.

Understanding the Literal Approach

I was once interviewed by the *Orange County Register*, a large newspaper in Southern California. The newspaper was running a story on angels. The reporter expressed incredulity that a modern Christian with a doctoral degree could possibly believe that references to angels in the Bible were to be taken literally. But I held my ground and affirmed that not only did I believe in them, but that Christ Himself believed in them. A plain reading of the biblical text allows for no other interpretation.

My friends, the literal meaning of Scripture embraces the standard, common understanding of each word in Scripture. Words in the Bible have the meaning they usually have in everyday communication. It is the basic or plain way of interpreting a passage.

So, contrary to the liberal Christian I told you about earlier, a plain reading of the second coming indicates that it will be a real event. *Christ will one day physically come again.* This is not an event that occurs over and over again as people find God again in their hearts. And when Christ comes, He will be accompanied by—*yes, you guessed it*—the angels! A plain reading of the biblical text allows for no other interpretation (Matthew 25:31).

I can think of at least six good reasons for adopting a literal interpretation of Scripture, including biblical prophecy:

1. A literal interpretation is the normal approach for understanding the meaning of all languages.

2. The greater part of the Bible makes good sense when taken literally.

3. A literal approach allows for metaphorical or symbolic meanings when the context calls for it. This is often the case in apocalyptic literature such as the books of Daniel and Revelation.

4. All metaphorical or symbolic meanings depend on the literal meaning. I humbly suggest you put on your thinking cap as you wrap your brain around the following sentence: We would not know *what is not* literally true unless we first understand *what is* literally true. (You might want to read that sentence a few times.) To illustrate, we would not know that Jesus is not literally a gate (John 10:9) unless we first know that He is a human being (John 1:14; Galatians 4:4). Because Jesus is *literally* a human being, we know He is *allegorically* a gate in the sense that He is the means of entering salvation.

5. The literal method is the only sane and safe check on the subjectively prone imagination of human beings.

6. The literal method is the only approach consistently in line with the idea that the very words of Scripture are "God-breathed" or inspired (2 Timothy 3:16). A symbolic approach to interpreting all Scripture undermines the idea that all Scripture originates from God.

We find several confirmations of the literal method of interpretation within the biblical text itself. Foundationally, later biblical texts take earlier ones as literal. Exodus 20:10-11, for example, takes the creation events in Genesis 1–2 quite literally.

OLD TESTAMENT EVENTS TAKEN LITERALLY IN THE NEW TESTAMENT	
The creation of Adam and Eve	Matthew 19:6; 1 Timothy 2:13
The fall of Adam and his resulting death	Romans 5:12,14
Noah's flood	Matthew 24:38
The account of Jonah	Matthew 12:40-42
The account of Moses	1 Corinthians 10:2-4,11

Further, over one hundred prophecies about the Messiah in the Old Testament found literal fulfillment with the first coming of Jesus Christ. These prophecies include that He would be from the seed of a woman (Genesis 3:15); from the line of Seth (Genesis 4:25); a descendant of Shem (Genesis 9:26); the offspring of Abraham (Genesis 12:3); from the tribe of Judah (Genesis 49:10); the son of David (Jeremiah 23:5-6); conceived of a virgin (Isaiah 7:14); born in Bethlehem (Micah 5:2); the Messiah (Isaiah 40:3); the coming King (Zechariah 9:9); the sacrificial offering for our sins (Isaiah 53); the one pierced in His side at the cross (Zechariah 12:10); predicted to die about AD 33 (Daniel 9:24-25); and raised from the dead (Psalm 2; 16). *Nothing allegorical here!*

MORE MESSIANIC PROPHECIES FULFILLED BY JESUS CHRIST		
Topic	OT Prophecy	Jesus Fulfills
Escape into Egypt	Hosea 11:1	Matthew 2:14
Immanuel	Isaiah 7:14	Matthew 1:23
Miracles	Isaiah 35:5-6	Matthew 9:35
Sold for 30 shekels	Zechariah 11:12	Matthew 26:15
Forsaken	Zechariah 13:7	Mark 14:50
Silent	Isaiah 53:7	Matthew 27:12-19
Hands/feet pierced	Psalm 22:16	John 20:25
Crucified	Isaiah 53:12	Matthew 27:38
No bones broken	Psalm 22:17	John 19:33-36
Suffered thirst	Psalm 69:21	John 19:28
Vinegar offered	Psalm 69:21	Matthew 27:34
Scourging/death	Isaiah 53:5	John 19:1,18
His "forsaken" cry	Psalm 22:1	Matthew 27:46
Ascension	Psalm 68:18	Luke 24:50-53
Right hand of God	Psalm 110:1	Hebrews 1:3

I always remind people that if they want to understand how God will fulfill prophecies of the future, consider how He already fulfilled prophecies in the past. God is perfectly consistent. The prophecies of Christ's first coming found literal fulfillment. The prophecies of Christ's second coming—and the events that lead up to it—will likewise find literal fulfillment.

There are a few other observations worth noting. First, by explicitly identifying parables (Matthew 13:3) and allegories (Galatians 4:24) within the text, the Bible shows that the ordinary meaning is literal. And by providing the interpretation of a parable, Jesus revealed there is a literal meaning behind each parable (Matthew 13:18-23).

We can also observe that Jesus rebuked Jewish leaders who did not interpret the resurrection literally. He thereby showed that the literal interpretation of the Old Testament was the correct one (Matthew

22:29-32; see also Psalms 2 and 16). Jesus's consistent literal interpretation of Old Testament Scripture—including prophetic Old Testament Scripture—is one of the most convincing pieces of evidence for a literal approach to Scripture.

Literalism is certainly the only approach consistent with God's purpose in creating human language. When God created Adam in His rational image, He gave Adam the gift of intelligible speech. This enabled him to communicate objectively with his Creator and with other human beings (Genesis 1:26; 11:1,7). Scripture shows that God sovereignly used human language as a medium of revelation, often through the "Thus saith the Lord" pronouncements of the prophets (Isaiah 7:7; 10:24; 22:15).

If God created language to communicate with humans—and to enable humans to communicate with each other—He would undoubtedly intend an ordinary and everyday sense of the words. This view of language is a prerequisite to understanding not only God's spoken word but His written Word (Scripture).

The Literal Approach and Symbols

The literal method does not eliminate the use of symbols. The Bible often uses symbols. But each symbol points to something literal. We see this illustrated in the book of Revelation.

SYMBOLS REPRESENT LITERAL THINGS	
John said the "seven stars" in Christ's right hand represent "the angels of the seven churches."	Revelation 1:20
John said the "seven gold lampstands" represent "the seven churches."	Revelation 1:20
John said the "gold bowls filled with incense" represent "the prayers of God's people."	Revelation 5:8
John said "the waters" represent "masses of people of every nation and language."	Revelation 17:15

We conclude that each symbol in Revelation represents something literal.
There are often textual clues that point us to the literal truth found in a
symbol. These textual clues may be found either in the immediate context or in the broader context of the whole of Scripture.

The Literal Approach and Figures of Speech

The literal method does not eliminate figures of speech. When the
Bible speaks of the eyes, arms, or wings of God (Psalm 34:15; Isaiah
51:9; Psalm 91:4), we do not take these as literally true. God does not
have these physical features since He is pure Spirit (John 4:24). Likewise, He cannot literally be a rock (Psalm 42:9), which is material. God
is a rock in the figurative sense of being our rock-solid foundation.

I grant that it may sometimes be challenging to determine when a
passage is literal. But specific guidelines help us make this determina-
tion. Briefly put, we should understand a text figuratively—

- when it is obviously figurative, as when Jesus said He was a
  gate (John 10:9)
- when the text itself provides a clue, such as "this may be
  interpreted allegorically" (Galatians 4:24 esv)
- when a literal interpretation would contradict other truths
  inside or outside the Bible, such as when the Bible speaks
  of the "four corners of the earth" (Revelation 7:1).

Bible expositor David Cooper provides this excellent summary:
"Take every word at its primary, ordinary, usual, literal meaning, unless
the facts of the immediate context, studied in the light of related
passages and axiomatic and fundamental truths, indicate clearly
otherwise."[3]

The Literal Approach and Jesus's Parables

The literal method does not eliminate the use of parables. Jesus
often used parables that He did not intend as literal. Yet, each parable
always conveys a literal point.

That Jesus wanted His parables to be clear to those who were recep-
tive is evident in how He carefully interpreted two of them for the

disciples—the parable of the sower (Matthew 13:3-9) and the parable of the tares (13:24-30). He did this not only so there would be no uncertainty about their correct meaning, but to guide believers as to the proper method to use in interpreting the other parables. That Christ did not interpret His subsequent parables shows that He fully expected believers to understand the literal truths intended by His parables by following the method He illustrated for them.

The Big Ideas

- Because prophecies in the past found literal fulfillment, we have good reason to believe prophecies of the future will find literal fulfillment.

- The greater part of the Bible makes good sense when taken literally.

- The literal method of interpreting prophecy allows for symbols, figures of speech, and parables, when clearly indicated in the context.

Questions for Reflection

1. Are you convinced God will literally fulfill prophecies of the future just as He did prophecies in the past? Why?

2. Have you ever thought about how subjective the allegorical approach is? Five allegorical interpreters could suggest five different interpretations of the same prophetic verse. Why might Satan like to promote allegorism?

3. Have you ever thanked God for His clear revelations in the Bible? Where would we be without them? Why not take a moment right now to thank Him?

5

How Can We Properly Interpret Bible Prophecy?

A pilot was flying a Cessna 172 single-engine plane, and in the passenger seat was an eighty-one-year-old man. They were flying from Indianapolis to Muncie, Indiana.

Suddenly, the pilot slumped over dead. The plane turned downward and nosedived. The stunned passenger immediately got on the radio and begged for anyone listening to help him.

Two nearby pilots heard the call. They gave the older man a steady stream of calm, precise instructions regarding climbing, steering, and the scariest part—landing the plane.

Emergency vehicles went out to the runway. Airport officials were expecting a disaster. But by following the precise rules provided by the two experienced pilots, the older man successfully touched down on the runway. It was not a pretty landing—the plane bounced on the runway before skidding into a patch of soggy grass. But the man followed the rules and successfully escaped serious injury.

Rules are important!

> **If you want to successfully interpret Bible prophecy, it is important to follow the rules of interpretation. Otherwise you might find yourself nosediving into imbalanced ideas about Bible prophecy.**

A rule-based interpreter "correctly explains the word of truth" (2 Timothy 2:15). I love this verse. It has a depth and richness in the original Greek that does not quite come across in English translations. Thomas Constable tells us that the original Greek "paints a picture of a workman who is careful and accurate in his work. The Greek word elsewhere describes a tent maker who makes straight rather than wavy cuts in his material. It pictures a builder who lays bricks in straight rows and a farmer who plows a straight furrow."[4]

Just as a workman is exceedingly precise and careful in his work, so you and I must be exceedingly precise and careful in interpreting Scripture. That is why interpretive principles are so beneficial. Following are seven of the more important ones that have guided me through the years.

1. Always Seek the Plain Sense

This is *the* foundational principle I have always used in interpreting Bible prophecy. I will remind you of it several times throughout this book.

> When the plain sense makes good sense, seek no other sense lest you end up in nonsense.

David Cooper suggests that given this dictum, we ought to "take every word at its primary, ordinary, usual, literal meaning, unless the facts of the immediate context...indicate clearly otherwise."[5] Likewise, Arnold Fruchtenbaum suggests that "unless the text indicates clearly that it should be taken symbolically, the passage should be understood literally"[6]—that is, in its *plain sense* (see chapter 4).

A relevant example relates to the specific promises God has made to Israel, including the land promises in the Abrahamic covenant (Genesis 12:1-3; 15:18-21; 17:21; 35:10-12). The plain sense of these verses makes perfect sense. There is no good reason to suppose—as replacement theologians do—that the church replaces Israel, and that promises made to Israel will find some kind of spiritual fulfill-ment in the church.

Always seek the plain sense.

2. Make Sure Your "Preunderstandings" Line Up with Scripture

A preunderstanding is an idea we have already formed based on previous experience. To illustrate, I used to live in Southern Cali-fornia, south of Los Angeles and north of San Diego. My wife and I visited a Mexican restaurant in the area. The salsa the waiter pro-vided tasted like diluted ketchup. *Not good!* We soon visited another Mexican restaurant in the area, and the salsa likewise had much to be desired. We soon developed a preunderstanding that Southern California does not have any good Mexican restaurants. This pre-understanding was eventually proven wrong with the third Mexi-can restaurant we visited. *The salsa was perfecto!*

A *theological* preunderstanding is a doctrinal opinion we have previously formed based on previous study of God's Word, Chris-tian books, denominational literature, sermons we've heard, and Christian leaders we've seen on TV or heard on radio. In inter-preting God's Word, it is important for us to submit all of our theological preunderstandings to the authority of Scripture. *Our preunderstandings could be wrong.* We should be cautious to avoid letting our preunderstandings bias our interpretation of individual Scripture verses.

I cannot overstate the importance of this. All interpreters have at least some theological and denominational prejudices. It is there-fore wise to ensure that our preunderstandings are in harmony with Scripture and are *subject to correction by it.* Only those preunder-standings fully compatible with Scripture are legitimate. We must always be open to modifying and reshaping our presuppositions and preunderstandings, given what we learn from the biblical text.

An example might be the preunderstanding held by many today that when the antichrist emerges on the scene, he will be a Mus-lim. These Bible interpreters have a theological bias in favor of this position, mainly because of the widely reported radical Islamic terrorism that is so prevalent in the world today.

Testing this preunderstanding against Scripture reveals significant problems. Daniel 9:26, for example, predicts the destruction of Jerusalem in AD 70 and also mentions the antichrist: "The people of the prince who is to come shall destroy the city and the sanctuary" (ESV). Contextually, the "prince who is to come" is the antichrist. The "people" who destroyed Jerusalem and its temple were the Romans. Since the antichrist is of this people, the antichrist will be a Roman Gentile and not a Muslim.

Make every effort to test ALL your preunderstandings against Scripture.

3. Pay Close Attention to the Context

The Bible student must ever pay close attention to the context when interpreting Scripture. Here is something you need to burn into your consciousness:

Every *word* in the Bible is part of a sentence.
Every *sentence* in the Bible is part of a paragraph.
Every *paragraph* in the Bible is part of a book.
Every *book* in the Bible is part of the whole of Scripture.

My friends, the interpretation of any single Bible verse must not contradict the total teaching of Scripture. *Individual verses do not exist as isolated fragments.* They are parts of a whole. This means our understanding of individual verses must be tested and clarified by our broader understanding of what the whole of Scripture teaches. I often tell students that *Scripture interprets Scripture.*

An example of the importance of context is Matthew 24:34, where Jesus said: "I tell you the truth, this generation will not pass from the scene until all these things take place." Did Jesus mean that all end-time prophecies would find fulfillment in *His* generation, as some today hold?

Consulting the context answers the question. Contextually, Christ affirmed that the generation that witnesses the signs He stated just earlier—the desecration of the Jewish temple (verse 15) and the rise of the great tribulation (verse 21), for example—will not pass until the remaining end-time prophecies find fulfillment. Since the tribulation will last seven years at the end of the age (Daniel 9:27; Revelation 11:2), Jesus is here revealing that the people alive at the beginning of the tribulation will still be alive at its end. *That* is the generation He was referring to.

Context clarifies the correct meaning of the text.

4. Make a Correct Genre Judgment

Accurately interpreting Scripture requires that we make a correct genre judgment. That might sound a little deep, but it is really not. I promise.

The Bible contains a variety of literary genres. For example, there are historical books (like the book of Acts), dramatic epics (like the book of Job), poetry (like the Psalms), wise sayings (like the book of Proverbs), and apocalyptic books (like the books of Daniel and Revelation). Each genre has its unique characteristics. An awareness of these characteristics makes it much easier for us to properly interpret Bible books.

Please allow me to give you a few examples. Biblical poetry contains many symbols that speak figuratively of God and other subjects. A case in point is how the Psalms refer to God as having wings:

> Have mercy on me, O God, have mercy!
>> I look to you for protection.
> I will hide beneath the shadow of your wings
>> until the danger passes by.
>> (Psalm 57:1)

The term *wings* is not intended to be taken literally. It is simply a symbolic way of speaking about God's protective presence. The Psalms—in the genre of poetry—often use such metaphors. An awareness of that fact helps me to interpret the Psalms rightly.

The book of Revelation is an apocalyptic genre that also includes many symbols. Unlike the Psalms, however, the book of Revelation typically defines the symbols for us. As noted previously in the book, "the seven lampstands" are identified as symbols of "the seven churches" (Revelation 1:20). The "gold bowls filled with incense" are identified as symbols of "the prayers of God's people" (5:8). An awareness of how apocalyptic books often contain symbolic language helps me to interpret Revelation and Daniel correctly.

That said, here is a critically important point you should remember:

> Even though the Bible contains a variety
> of literary genres, some of which include
> symbols, the biblical authors most often used
> literal statements to convey their ideas.

Where the Bible writers use a literal means to express their ideas, the Bible student must use a literal approach in interpreting those ideas. A literal method of interpreting Scripture gives to each word in the text the same basic meaning it would have in normal, ordinary, customary usage—whether used in writing, speaking, or thinking. Without such a method, communication between God and man would be impossible.

To illustrate, the prophetic promise in 1 Thessalonians 4:15-16 is a literal statement of truth from the apostle Paul. It is not intended to be symbolic. Paul here affirms: "First, the believers who have died will rise from their graves. Then, together with them, we who are still alive and remain on the earth will be caught up in the clouds to meet the Lord in the air. Then we will be with the Lord forever." *This will one day really happen!* To allegorize this passage would constitute forcing a false meaning into Scripture.

In sum, the wise interpreter allows his knowledge of genres to control how he approaches each biblical text. In this way, he can accurately determine what the biblical author intended to communicate to the reader.

5. Consult History and Culture

Another important rule of interpretation involves consulting biblical history and culture. The Bible student should make every effort to step out of his or her Western mindset and into an ancient Jewish mindset. He or she must pay particular attention to such things as Jewish marriage rites, burial rites, family practices, farm practices, business practices, the monetary system, methods of warfare, slavery, the treatment of captives, the use of covenants, and religious practices. Armed with such detailed historical information, interpreting the Bible correctly becomes a much easier task because we better understand the world and culture of the biblical writers.

Have you ever wondered why the antichrist is called a "small horn" in Daniel 8:9? An understanding of biblical history and culture sheds light on the issue.

The ancient Jews recognized that a horned animal used its horn as a weapon (see Genesis 22:13; Psalm 69:31). For this reason, the horn eventually became a symbol of power and might among the Jews. As an extension of this symbol, it became an emblem of dominion—representing kingdoms and kings—as in the books of Daniel and Revelation (see Daniel 7–8; Revelation 12:13; 13:1,11; 17:3-16). We can therefore surmise that the antichrist, as a "small horn," apparently emerges with localized dominion, and only later attains global dominion (Revelation 13).

6. Be Mindful of the Law of Double Reference

Here is a rule you probably have not heard of, but it is still important. According to the law of double reference, a single passage of prophetic Scripture may refer to two events separated by a significant time period. Both prophesied events blend into one picture, masking the intervening time period. While the time gap may not be clear in the text, it becomes evident in consultation with other verses.

To illustrate the law of double reference, I might say to someone on a Monday morning, "Our pastor next Sunday will be speaking on the role of husbands in marriage as well as the role of wives in marriage." That statement could easily be taken to mean that the pastor will speak of all this in a single sermon. In reality, he will speak of the role of the husband in marriage during next Sunday's morning service and the role of wives in the evening service. My statement thus contains a double reference. While the time gap is not evident in my statement, any confusion of the matter is cleared up by consulting the church bulletin.

The law of double reference is especially important when we consider Old Testament prophecies about the coming of Christ. The question that emerges is this: Does the prophecy in a particular Scripture verse find complete fulfillment in the first coming of Christ alone, or does it also point to the second coming of Christ? Consider Zechariah 9:9-10 as an example:

> Rejoice, O people of Zion!
>> Shout in triumph, O people of Jerusalem!
> Look, your king is coming to you.
>> He is righteous and victorious,
> yet he is humble, riding on a donkey—
>> riding on a donkey's colt...
> His realm will stretch from sea to sea
>> and from the Euphrates River to the ends of the earth.

These verses speak of both Christ's *first* coming (riding on a donkey) and His *second* coming, which will issue in His universal millennial reign that will extend "from sea to sea...to the ends of the earth." (See Isaiah 11:1-5 for another example.)

7. Watch for Insights About Jesus
From beginning to end—from Genesis to Revelation—the

Bible is a Jesus book. Jesus once told some Jews, "You search the Scriptures because you think they give you eternal life. But the Scriptures point to me! Yet you refuse to come to me to receive this life" (John 5:39-40).

Luke 24 speaks of the resurrected Jesus appearing to two disciples on the road to Emmaus: "Jesus took them through the writings of Moses and all the prophets, explaining from all the Scriptures the things concerning himself" (Luke 24:27). Jesus also affirmed that the Scriptures were "written about me" (Luke 24:44; see also Hebrews 10:7). *Jesus is the heart and center of Scripture.*

This means the interpreter of Bible prophecy must always look for Jesus in the text. The fancy theological term for this is that our interpretation of prophetic Scripture must be *Christocentric* (centered on Christ).

THE CHRISTOCENTRIC NATURE OF BIBLE PROPHECY	
Jesus is building a place for us to live in heaven: the New Jerusalem.	John 14:1-3; Revelation 21
Jesus will come for us at the rapture.	1 Thessalonians 4:13-17
Jesus will preside over the judgment of Christians in heaven.	2 Corinthians 5:10
Jesus will inflict judgments upon the people on earth during the tribulation period.	Revelation 6
Jesus will come again at the second coming.	Revelation 19:11-21
Jesus will judge the nations.	Matthew 25:31-46
Jesus will reign during His millennial kingdom.	Revelation 20:2-5
Jesus will preside over the judgment of the wicked dead.	Revelation 20:11-15

To truly understand Bible prophecy, always be on the lookout for Jesus.

The Big Ideas

- When the plain sense makes good sense, seek no other sense lest you end up in nonsense.

- Always be ready to modify any preunderstandings you have based on what you learn from Scripture.

- Consider the context of every verse, remembering that *Scripture interprets Scripture.*

- Be mindful that different genres in the Bible have different characteristics.

- Consult biblical history and culture for background insights on Bible verses.

- Maintain a constant awareness of the law of double reference.

- Watch for Jesus in prophecy verses, for the Bible is *Christocentric.*

Questions for Reflection

1. In view of the Bible being a "Jesus book," can you think of any insights about Jesus in the Psalms? If you are having trouble, compare Psalm 23 with John 10:1-16 and Hebrews 13:20.

2. Can you think of how this role of Jesus relates to prophecy? (Revelation 7:17 might help you.)

6

How Can We Avoid
Prophetic Imbalances?

When my kids were learning to drive, I felt it essential for them to learn all the rules of safe driving. They needed to learn the right way to drive, which included teaching them about specific things to avoid. For example, when driving, one should avoid speeding, driving when sleepy, taking eyes off the road, icy roads, and sending text messages on a smartphone.

When studying Bible prophecy, one must not only learn the right way to interpret it, but also learn things to avoid. Based on many years of experience, I suggest there are seven things that are especially important to avoid when studying prophecy.

1. Avoid Prophetic Agnosticism

Agnosticism is another one of those big words professors like to use in seminaries. But don't let it intimidate you. The word derives from two Greek words: *a*, meaning "no" or "without," and *gnosis*, meaning "knowledge." Agnosticism simply means "no knowledge" or "without knowledge."

Strictly speaking, an agnostic is a person who claims he is unsure—having "no knowledge"—about spiritual matters, especially the existence of God. Agnosticism is prevalent in the world today, embracing about 16 percent of the world's population.

When I travel abroad, sometimes a friend might treat me by taking me to his favorite restaurant. I always confess to my friend that I am sometimes a culinary agnostic. By this I mean *I am not sure* I will enjoy eating something I have never heard of. I have *no knowledge* whether my taste buds will react favorably to ingredients I have never eaten before. In most cases, my culinary agnosticism quickly vanishes with what turns out to be a delicious meal.

A prophetic agnostic is a person who says, "I am unsure about Bible prophecy." Such a person has doubts about whether Bible prophecy is accurate or trustworthy.

Some people become prophetic agnostics because they think Bible prophecy is too difficult or complicated to understand. Others point to failed date predictions of prophecies set forth by well-meaning but undiscerning (and unbiblical) Christians. Because of dashed hopes, many conclude we cannot be sure of what the future holds.

I urge you not to fall prey to this attitude. Over one-fourth of the Bible was prophetic when originally written. That is too much of the Bible to be unsure about. You are holding in your hands a book that will dispel prophetic agnosticism. If you have ever been unsure about prophecy—or have had doubts about its trustworthiness—please keep reading.

2. Avoid Prophetic Sensationalism

Sensationalism involves the use of exciting or shocking stories or language at the expense of accuracy to provoke public interest or excitement in something. *Prophetic* sensationalism consists of using exciting or shocking stories or language about prophecy at the expense of accuracy to provoke public interest or excitement in prophecy.

An example is how some prophecy enthusiasts have claimed that references to prophetic signs in the sky (Joel 2:30; Luke 21:15) may refer to visitations from UFOs, and that perhaps the aliens aboard these UFOs are the Nephilim mentioned in Genesis 6. That is a pretty sensational claim guaranteed to grab people's attention. It sure grabbed my attention. But is there any substantial evidence for it? I have not seen any.

Another example of sensationalism is the "drill to hell" scam that emerged in the 1990s. A geological group in Siberia allegedly drilled a hole in the ground nine miles deep. When they dropped a microphone down the hole, they reportedly heard people screaming in agony in hell. Again, that is a sensational claim guaranteed to grab people's attention. It made headlines around the world. But is there any real evidence for it? Is it accurate? *No!*

We must avoid such sensationalism when studying Bible prophecy. Christ calls His followers to live soberly and alertly as they await His coming. In fact, in Mark 13:33, Jesus spoke about His second coming and then urged His followers to "be on guard! Stay alert!" First Peter 4:7 instructs: "The end of all things is at hand; therefore be self-controlled and sober-minded" (ESV). The Amplified Bible translates this verse, "The end and culmination of all things has now come near; keep sound minded and self-restrained." The New American Standard Bible translates it, "The end of all things is near; therefore, be of sound judgment and sober spirit."

Here is something you'll want to remember:

> As we consider prophetic events, we should avoid sensationalism and instead be "on guard," "alert," "self-controlled," "sober-minded," "sound-minded," "self-restrained," and of "sound judgment." Keep a level head.

3. Avoid Newspaper Exegesis

Newspaper exegesis involves having a newspaper in one hand and the Bible in the other, forcing headlines from the newspaper into the text of prophetic Scripture. An example might be how some Christians used to read newspaper headlines about President Barack Obama and force them into prophecies about the antichrist, concluding that he was, in fact, the antichrist.

Christians ought never to practice such newspaper exegesis. The proper approach is first to study the Scriptures to find out what God has revealed about the prophetic future. We can then measure current events against what the Bible reveals about the future to give thoughtful consideration as to whether there is a *legitimate* correlation (see Matthew 16:1-3; Luke 21:29-33). We ought never force newspaper headlines into prophetic Scripture.

Arnold Fruchtenbaum suggests that "current events must never be the means of interpreting the Scriptures, but the Scriptures must interpret current events."[7] Mark Hitchcock puts it similarly: "When considering signs of the times, we must make sure that we view current events in light of the Bible and not the other way around."[8]

4. Avoid Setting Dates for Prophetic Events

I hate to say it, but many Christians through the years have tried to attach specific dates to prophetic events. Here's a brief survey:

DATE-SETTING	RESULT
Edgar C. Whisenant claimed the rapture would occur on September 11, 12, or 13, 1988.	It didn't happen.
When Whisenant's date of the rapture failed, he altered the date to October 3, 1988.	It didn't happen.
Harold Camping claimed Jesus would return in September 1994.	It didn't happen.
Camping later prophesied that Jesus would come for His own on May 21, 2011.	It didn't happen.
Mary Stewart Relfe claimed the second coming of Christ would occur in 1997.	It didn't happen.

There are good reasons Christians ought to avoid setting dates for specific prophetic events. First, over the past two thousand years, the track record of those who have predicted or expected "the end" have been 100 percent wrong. The history of doomsday predictions is little more than a history of dashed expectations. Though I believe there is a strong likelihood that we are today living in the season of the Lord's coming for us at the rapture, it is also a possibility that the rapture is still a long way off. Guessing a date for the rapture or any other prophetic event is therefore foolish. Let's resist the temptation.

Second, a Christian who sets dates might make harmful decisions for his or her life. Selling one's possessions and heading for the mountains, going off to join a survivalist sect, spending a lot of money to purchase a bomb shelter, stopping the educational process, choosing to not save money for retirement, choosing not to buy health insurance or life insurance, leaving family and friends—these are destructive actions that might potentially ruin one's life.

Third, Christians who succumb to believing in specific dates for prophetic events might damage their faith when their expectations fail. Such Christians may also find their overall confidence in the Bible waning, all because of misplaced and unbiblical hopes.

Fourth, if one loses confidence in the prophetic portions of Scripture due to a failed prophetic date, then biblical prophecy may cease to be a motivation to personal purity and holiness in daily life (see Titus 2:12-14; 2 Peter 3:11; 1 John 3:2-3).

Fifth, date-setting damages the cause of Christ. Humanists, skeptics, atheists, and secularists enjoy scornfully pointing to Christians who have put stock in end-time predictions—especially when they suggest specific dates for these events. They love to write articles about "those gullible Christians." Why give ammo to those who are antagonistic to Christianity?

Finally, the timing of end-time events is entirely in God's hands, and He has not given us the exact specifics on timing. Jesus told His followers, "The Father alone has the authority to set those dates and times, and they are not for you to know" (Acts 1:7).

I see nothing wrong with Christians being excited that we are living in the end times. But let's not set dates.

Here is my best advice on the matter:

Let's *live* our lives as if the Lord could come
for us today but *plan* our lives as if we'll be
here our entire life expectancy. That way,
we are prepared for time and eternity.

5. Avoid Confusing Israel and the Church

This is a topic of big-time controversy! Some Christians—largely those who allegorize Bible prophecy—are open to the idea that prophetic promises made to Israel in Old Testament times are somehow fulfilled in a spiritual way in the church. Other Christians—those who take a literal approach to Bible prophecy (such as yours truly)—believe that Israel and the church are distinct, and that God has specific plans for each.

Here is the way I see it:

First, Israel and the church are similar in some important ways:

- Both are part of the people of God.
- Both are part of God's spiritual kingdom.
- And both take part in the spiritual blessings of the Abrahamic and new covenants.

These are significant similarities.

Without minimizing the importance of such similarities, Scripture also portrays Israel and the church as distinct from each other in at least four ways:

1. The roots of Israel predate the time of Moses in Old Testament times. The church began on the day of Pentecost in New Testament times (Acts 1:5; 1 Corinthians 12:13).

2. Israel is an earthly political entity (Exodus 19:5-6). The universal church is the invisible spiritual body of Christ (Ephesians 1:3).

3. One becomes a Jew by physical birth. One becomes a member of the church via a spiritual birth (or rebirth—being "born again") through personal faith in Jesus Christ (John 3:3,16).

4. While Israel consists of Jews, the church consists of both redeemed Jews and Gentiles (see Ephesians 2:15).

Prophetic Scripture reveals that God still has a plan for national Israel. That plan includes allowing Israel to go through the tribulation period (unlike the church), during which God will purge Israel as a means of motivating the nation to repent of its rejection of Jesus (Zechariah 13:8-9). At the very end of the tribulation period, a remnant of Jews will repent and turn to Jesus for salvation (Romans 9–11). Following the second coming, redeemed Jews will be invited into Christ's millennial kingdom (Ezekiel 20:34-38). God will then fulfill promises He has made to Israel. God will give Israel the land promised in the Abrahamic covenant (Genesis 12:1-3; 15:18-21; 17:21; 35:10-12). He will also fulfill the throne promise in the Davidic covenant, as Christ rules on the throne of David throughout the millennial kingdom (2 Samuel 7:5-17).

Meanwhile, as noted, it is not God's purpose for the church to go through the tribulation period. God has promised to deliver the church from the wrath to come (1 Thessalonians 1:10; 5:9; see also Romans 5:9). The church will be raptured off the earth prior to the beginning of the tribulation period (1 Thessalonians 4:13-18; Revelation 3:10).

Now, at this juncture I need to give you a heads-up on a matter that might seem just a tad complicated. You might want to slip on your thinking cap for a moment. Here it is in the form of a question: *Even though God has distinct plans for Israel and the church, what happens if a Jew becomes a Christian in the current church age?*

The answer is rather simple. God still has a plan for *national* Israel. But if an *individual* Jew places faith in Christ during the current church age, that Jewish person is absorbed into the body of Christ, thereby becoming a part of the church (Romans 10:12-13; Galatians 3:28). Just because an individual Jew might become a Christian and a member of the church does not in any way negate God's broader promises to *national* Israel. God will fulfill all that has been promised to Israel (Romans 9–11).

> Remember what I said previously in the book: God is a promise-keeper (Numbers 23:19; Deuteronomy 7:9; Joshua 21:45; 23:14; 1 Kings 8:56)!

6. Avoid Confusion Over God's Multiple Judgments

Scripture speaks of the judgment *of Christians* following the rapture (1 Corinthians 3:10-15; 2 Corinthians 5:10), the judgment *of the nations* following the second coming of Christ (Joel 3:2; Matthew 25:31-46), the judgment *of the Jews* following the second coming of Christ (Ezekiel 20:34-38), and the judgment *of the wicked* at the great white throne judgment following Christ's thousand-year millennial kingdom (Revelation 20:12). Some prophecy enthusiasts—especially those who take a more allegorical approach to interpreting prophecy— try to merge all these judgments into one big judgment at the end.

I do not think it is wise to do this. Second Timothy 2:15 urges "accurately handling and skillfully teaching the word of truth" (AMP), or as the King James Version puts it, "rightly dividing the word of truth." My friends, rightly dividing the word of truth requires viewing these judgments as distinct from each other.

Please allow me to illustrate this by comparing the *judgment of the nations* and the *great white throne judgment*:

COMPARISON	JUDGMENT OF THE NATIONS	GREAT WHITE THRONE JUDGMENT
Different Time	Occurs at the second coming of Christ (Matthew 25:31)	Occurs following Christ's thousand-year millennial kingdom (Revelation 20:11-12)
Different Scene	Occurs on earth (Matthew 25:31)	Occurs at the great white throne, away from the earth (Revelation 20:11)
Different Subjects	Three groups present: the sheep, the goats, and the brothers (Matthew 25:32,40)	Only one group is present: the unsaved dead of all time (Revelation 20:12)
Different Basis	One's personal treatment of Christ's "brothers" during the tribulation period (Matthew 25:40)	One's works throughout earthly life (Revelation 20:12)
Different Result	The righteous enter Christ's millennial kingdom; the unrighteous suffer eternal punishment (Matthew 25:46)	The wicked enter the lake of fire; the righteous are not mentioned, for they are not present (Revelation 20:14)
Resurrection	No resurrection is mentioned	The wicked dead are resurrected prior to judgment (Revelation 20:13)

A plain reading of the biblical text shows that these judgments are not the same. They are distinct in many ways. Biblically, there are *distinct* judgments of Christians, the nations, the Jews, and the wicked.

Let us commit to rightly dividing the word of truth.

7. Avoid Dividing with Other Christians

Christians hold a variety of opinions on many issues related to biblical prophecy. On the doctrine of the rapture alone, some believers believe it happens *before* the tribulation period, others at the *midpoint* of the tribulation period, and still others *after* the tribulation period. Even though we debate some of the finer points of Bible prophecy, it is important to note that we agree on a lot of the big stuff:

THE BIG STUFF WE ALL AGREE ON
Christ is coming again.
We will all receive incredible body upgrades (resurrection bodies).
We are accountable and will face judgment for how we lived on earth.
As Christians, we will live forever with God face-to-face.
In the afterlife there will be no more sin, suffering, Satan, or death.

Staying aware of the big stuff we all agree on helps us to keep everything in proper perspective. Even amid our minor debates, we need not have divisive attitudes. When interpreting prophecy, we all need a good dose of humility to temper our leanings toward dogmatism.

Given that human beings are finite and fallible, it is understandable that there will be differences of opinion—especially on nonessential matters (such as the exact timing of the rapture). There is no reason that each of us cannot hold our own cherished view on the specific issues of Bible prophecy—*and even become fully convinced that we are right on the matter.* There is good reason, however, that none of these nonessential teachings should be a test of orthodoxy or Christian fellowship.

Regardless of whether all Christians are in full agreement with me on issues related to prophecy, my primary identity centers on being a Christian who loves all other Christians. Even when I express my differing views to other Christians, I want to do it lovingly.

This means it is not merely *what we believe* but *how we behave* that is important. Jesus emphasized the importance of truth. He said, "You will know the truth, and the truth will set you free" (John 8:32). But He also said that love is the distinguishing mark of a Christian (John 13:35). One can be right in what he says and wrong in the way he says it.

I love the writings of J.C. Ryle. In his classic book *Holiness*, he notes how hurtful words can be among Christians who disagree with each other, and how such hurtful words are self-defeating: "I must enter my protest against the sneering, taunting, contemptuous language which has been frequently used of late...To say the least, such language is unseemly, and only defeats its own end. A cause which is defended by such language is deservedly suspicious. Truth needs no such weapons. If we cannot agree with men, we need not speak of their views with discourtesy and contempt."[9] Ryle thus urges: "Let us exercise charity in our judgments of one another," noting that to "exhibit bitterness and coldness" toward those who disagree with us on some matter "is to prove ourselves very ignorant of real holiness."[10]

J.I. Packer helps us to understand the importance of charitable behavior in the body of Christ using a metaphor of a family:

> How ought families—siblings, specifically brothers and sisters—to behave? Well, you are not going to deny that siblings ought to act like and look like parts of a family. If brothers and sisters never meet together, never speak to each other, appear to be entirely indifferent to each other— that is an unnatural and scandalous state. That would be true of any human family. I put it to you without fear of contradiction: the same is true of the family of God.[11]

Packer's point is that "divisions in the church which prevent the family from acting like one family and the body from functioning like one body...are unnatural; unnatural to the point of being shameful."[12] The better way is the way of love and charity.

I think the apostle Paul struck the perfect balance when he exhorted the Ephesians about the importance of "speaking the truth in love" (Ephesians 4:15). Paul was a profound defender of the truth, but he was always loving.

I close with a well-known but straightforward admonition:

> *In essentials, unity;*
> *in nonessentials, liberty;*
> *and in all things, charity.*

Speaking the truth in love may not always be easy, but it is the charitable thing to do!

The Big Ideas

- Avoid prophetic agnosticism.
- Avoid prophetic sensationalism.
- Avoid newspaper exegesis.
- Avoid setting dates for prophetic events.
- Avoid confusing Israel and the church.
- Avoid confusion over God's multiple judgments.
- Avoid dividing with other Christians.

Questions for Reflection

1. What would you say are the three most important things you learned in this chapter?

2. Do you agree with the maxim, "In essentials, unity; in nonessentials, liberty; and in all things, charity"? Do you want to make any changes in your life in view of this maxim?

PART 2

WHO ARE THE PRIMARY PERSONALITIES OF THE END TIMES?

7

Who Are the Bad Guys?

People love to watch movies that feature heroic good guys and sinister bad guys. The same is true for TV dramas and novels. The better the good guys and the worse the bad guys, the better the story gets. And if the drama is based on real life, the interest level rises still further.

That is what makes the drama of the end times so fascinating. It features the best good guys and the worst bad guys you could ever imagine—*and it is all real-life drama.*

In this chapter, we will begin our exploration of the WHO of Bible prophecy. Remember—the WHO is just one vantage point in our much broader study of prophecy. Along with the other vantage points—the WHAT, WHEN, WHERE, and WHY—you will gain a full, composite understanding of Bible prophecy.

The professor of one of the graduate writing courses I took said that every great drama has a full and diverse cast of characters—both major and minor characters, both good guys and bad guys. The unfolding drama of the end times is no different.

The *good guys*, of course, are the righteous. They are on God's side.

The *bad guys* are the wicked. They are on the side of Satan and the antichrist.

Before I zero in on the details, please allow me to give you the big picture of how *all* the characters—the good guys, the bad guys, and the invisible spirit world—interrelate with each other. Pay special attention to the **words in bold type.** These are the cast of characters I will address in this and the following two chapters.

The End-Times Cast of Characters

Israel will continue to be a sore spot in the world in the end times. Many Muslim countries will increasingly want to see **Israel** destroyed. One day, a **massive northern military coalition**—comprising Muslim nations working alongside Russia—will launch a massive invasion against **Israel**. The leader of this invasion will be a czar-like figure known as **Gog**. **God** Himself will destroy **Gog** and the **invading forces**. This will take place either before the tribulation period or at the very beginning of it.

Meanwhile, the last days will involve hard times in other ways, with the number of **hardened sinners** escalating worldwide. There will be tremendous religious deception with the widespread proliferation of **false messiahs, false prophets**, and **false teachers**. These **false messiahs** and **false prophets** will set the stage for the eventual emergence of the **antichrist** (the ultimate false messiah) and the ultimate **false prophet**, his right-hand man.

The **antichrist**, the **false prophet**, and **Satan** will be the three main bad guys of the tribulation period. The **antichrist** will start out heading up a revived Roman Empire, but he will eventually attain worldwide dominion. The **false prophet's** primary role will be to lead the world to worship the **antichrist**. Behind the scenes in the spiritual world, **Satan** will work through both the **antichrist** and the **false prophet**. **Demons**, under **Satan's** leadership, will also wreak havoc on the earth during these years.

None of this will be a surprise to **God**, who is omniscient, and who knows the end from the beginning. **The Father, Jesus Christ**, and **the Holy Spirit** will each play a role in the end times. **The Father** is the ultimate source of prophecy, and He is sovereign over all things—including the end times. **Jesus** is the ultimate revealer of prophecy, whether speaking through the prophets, preaching sermons, or in delivering the book of Revelation to John. Much of end-times prophecy centers on the person of **Jesus**. **The Holy Spirit** presently restrains the emergence of the **antichrist**, but that restraint will vanish at the rapture. **The Holy Spirit** will nevertheless remain on earth, bringing many to salvation during these horrific years.

Meanwhile, **God** will use His **holy angels** to engage in a variety of ministries, including:

- delivering prophetic messages
- announcing God's judgments
- executing those judgments
- gathering the wicked for judgment following the second coming

Despite the dark days ahead, **God** will ensure there will be His witnesses to the truth on the earth. This will include the **144,000 Jewish evangelists** who will preach the gospel of the kingdom worldwide. It will also include God's **two mighty prophetic witnesses** who will engage in miracles similar to those of Moses and Elijah. Through their efforts, along with the ministry of **the Holy Spirit, a great multitude** will become believers during the tribulation period.

The **Jewish remnant**, however, will remain in danger. The forces of the **antichrist** will move against the **Jewish remnant** at the very end of the tribulation period. Miraculously, **God** will remove the spiritual blindness of the **Jewish remnant**, and they will turn to **Jesus**, their Messiah. Their repentance will be genuine. Knowing they are in danger from the **antichrist**, they will call out to **Jesus** for deliverance. The second coming will promptly occur, and **Jesus** will deliver the **remnant**.

Following the second coming, **Jesus** will engage in the judgment of **the nations** (or Gentiles). Christ will separate **the sheep** (believing Gentiles) from **the goats** (unbelieving Gentiles). He will judge them based on how they treat **Christ's "brothers"** (the 144,000 Jewish evangelists) during the tribulation period.

Christ will then set up His millennial kingdom. He will invite **redeemed Jews** and **redeemed Gentiles** directly into the kingdom. He will exclude **unbelievers** and cast them into judgment. **The church**, previously raptured before the tribulation period, will reign with **Christ** during the millennial kingdom.

Having provided this concise summary of the end-times cast of characters, let's now narrow our attention to the sinister bad guys of the end times.

The Rise of Gog—Leader of the Northern Military Coalition Against Israel

The prophet Ezekiel prophesied twenty-six hundred years ago that God would regather the Jews from "many nations" to the land of Israel in the end times (Ezekiel 36–37). Israel became a nation again in 1948, and the Jews have been streaming back to Israel ever since.

Ezekiel then prophesied that, sometime later, there would be an all-out invasion of Israel by a massive northern assault force. Russia will head up a coalition of Muslim nations—Iran, Sudan, Turkey, Libya, and other Muslim nations—against Israel. Their goal will be to obliterate the Jews. The sheer size of this assault force will mean Israel will stand no chance of defending itself. God, however, will intervene and supernaturally destroy the invaders (Ezekiel 38–39).

REFERENCE IN EZEKIEL 38:1-6	MODERN COUNTRY
Rosh	Russia
Magog	Kazakhstan, Kyrgyzstan, Uzbekistan, Turkmenistan, Tajikistan, and Afghanistan
Meshech and Tubal, Gomer, and Beth-togarmah	Turkey
Persia	Iran
Ethiopia	Sudan
Put	Libya

The nations prophesied to join this alliance in the end times are already coming together in our day. The growing emergence of this alliance following Israel's rebirth as a nation in 1948 is prophetically significant. The stage is currently being set for the predicted invasion.

Gog is the leader of this end-times military coalition. This may or may not be a proper name. First Chronicles 5:4 refers to an altogether different Gog: "The descendants of Joel were Shemaiah, Gog, Shimei, Micah, Reaiah, Baal, and Beerah." This verse shows that "Gog" can be a proper name. It would seem, however, that the term is not a proper name in Ezekiel 38–39.

The term may refer to a king-like role—such as pharaoh, caesar, czar, or president. The term *Gog* literally means "high," "supreme," "a height," or "a high mountain." This czar-like military leader will be a man of great stature who commands tremendous respect.

Gog is not just another name for the antichrist. We will end up in prophetic chaos if we try to make this identification. The antichrist will head up a revived Roman Empire (Daniel 2 and 7), while Gog will lead an invasion force made up of Russia and Muslim nations (Ezekiel 38:1-6). Gog's invasion into Israel will be a direct challenge to the antichrist's covenant with Israel (Daniel 9:27). Further, Gog's moment in the limelight will be short-lived—it will be all over when God destroys the invading forces (Ezekiel 39). The antichrist, by contrast, will be in power over the greater part of the tribulation period.

Gog is a time-limited bad guy.

Increase of Hardened Sinners

Scripture prophesies that the number of hardened sinners will explode in the end times. This will make life exceedingly difficult on earth during this time. The apostle Paul in 2 Timothy 3:1-5 tells us:

> In the last days there will be very difficult times. For people will love only themselves and their money. They will be boastful and proud, scoffing at God, disobedient to their parents, and ungrateful. They will consider nothing sacred. They will be unloving and unforgiving; they will slander others and have no self-control. They will be cruel and hate what is good. They will betray their friends, be reckless, be puffed up with pride, and love pleasure rather than God. They will act religious, but they will reject the power that could make them godly.

Please notice that in the last days, people will love themselves (we might call this *humanism*). They will love money (we might call this *materialism*). They will also love pleasure (we might call this *hedonism*). Significantly, humanism, materialism, and hedonism are three of the most prominent philosophies in our world today. They complement each other.

In keeping with this, Jesus gave this prophetic warning about hardened sinners in the end times:

> "Sin will be rampant everywhere, and the love of many will grow cold...When the Son of Man returns, it will be like it was in Noah's day. In those days before the flood, the people were enjoying banquets and parties and weddings right up to the time Noah entered his boat. People didn't realize what was going to happen until the flood came and swept them all away. That is the way it will be when the Son of Man comes" (Matthew 24:12,37-39).

This passage refers explicitly to the future tribulation period. But we see the attitude Jesus described even in our day. People are merrily going about their way, seemingly with no concern for the things of God, and oblivious that judgment is on the horizon.

False Messiahs, False Prophets, and False Teachers

Scripture prophesies that there will be a great increase in false messiahs, false prophets, and false teachers in the end times. In his prophetic Olivet Discourse, Jesus warned:

> "Don't let anyone mislead you, for many will come in my name, claiming, 'I am the Messiah.' They will deceive many...And many false prophets will appear and will deceive many people...
>
> "Then if anyone tells you, 'Look, here is the Messiah,' or 'There he is,' don't believe it. For false messiahs and false prophets will rise up and perform great signs and wonders so as to deceive, if possible, even God's chosen ones. See, I have warned you about this ahead of time.

"So if someone tells you, 'Look, the Messiah is out in the desert,' don't bother to go and look. Or, 'Look, he is hiding here,' don't believe it!" (Matthew 24:5,11,23-26; compare with 2 Corinthians 11:4).

Jesus's words point to a pervasive escalation of deception in the end times. This is in keeping with the apostle Paul's end-time warnings. In 1 Timothy 4:1, Paul said: "The Holy Spirit tells us clearly that in the last times some will turn away from the true faith; they will follow deceptive spirits and teachings that come from demons." Such demonic spirits often speak through false prophets.

It is relevant that many of the cults and false religions that pepper the religious landscape today first emerged when the leaders of these groups received an alleged revelation from an "angel"—which we know to be demonic spirits. A classic example is Mormonism, founded by Joseph Smith after he received an alleged revelation from the angel Moroni. Another example is Islam, based on alleged revelations brought to Muhammad by "the angel Gabriel" (a demonic imposter). In both cases, the revelations that came from these spirits contradict the Bible in notable ways.

The apostle Paul also warned: "A time is coming when people will no longer listen to sound and wholesome teaching. They will follow their own desires and will look for teachers who will tell them whatever their itching ears want to hear. They will reject the truth and chase after myths" (2 Timothy 4:2-3). Such an undiscerning attitude opens the door for people to fall prey to false messiahs, false prophets, and false teachers.

The Antichrist

The apostle Paul warned of a "man of lawlessness," which is the antichrist (2 Thessalonians 2:3,8-9). This individual will perform counterfeit signs and wonders and deceive many people during the future tribulation period (2 Thessalonians 2:9-10). The apostle John describes him in the book of Revelation as "the beast" (Revelation 13:1-10).

While the Holy Spirit energized Christ (Luke 4:14), Satan (the *un*holy spirit) will energize the antichrist (2 Thessalonians 2:9; Revelation 13:4). It is therefore understandable that the antichrist takes on the characteristics of Satan:

Just as **Satan** is prideful and self-exalting (Isaiah 14:12-17; Ezekiel 28:11-19),	so **the antichrist** will be prideful and self-exalting (2 Thessalonians 2:4).
Just as **Satan** engages in great deception (John 8:44; Revelation 12:9),	so **the antichrist** will engage in great deception (2 Thessalonians 2:9-10).
Just as **Satan** engages in severe persecution against God's people (Revelation 12:12-17),	so **the antichrist** will engage in severe persecution against God's people (Revelation 13:7; Daniel 7:21).

The antichrist will rise to prominence in the tribulation period, initially making a peace treaty with Israel (Daniel 9:27). Soon after, he will seek to dominate the world, double-cross and then attempt to destroy the Jews, persecute believers, and set up his own kingdom (Revelation 13). He will speak arrogant and boastful words in glorifying himself (2 Thessalonians 2:4).

The antichrist's assistant, the false prophet, will seek to make the world worship the antichrist (Revelation 13:11-12). He will attempt to force people worldwide to receive "the mark of the beast," without which they cannot buy or sell. This squeeze play will enable the antichrist to control the global economy (Revelation 13:16-17). However, to receive this mark ensures one of being the recipient of God's wrath. The antichrist will eventually rule the entire world (Revelation 13:7), with his headquarters initially in Rome, later in Jerusalem, and still later in New Babylon (Revelation 17:8-9).

During the tribulation period, the antichrist will make every attempt to mimic the true Christ in multiple perverted ways:

CHRIST MIMICKED BY THE ANTICHRIST	
Christ	The Antichrist
Miracles, signs, and wonders (Matthew 9:32-33; Mark 6:2)	Miracles, signs, and wonders (2 Thessalonians 2:9)
Appears in the millennial temple (Ezekiel 43:6-7)	Sits in the tribulation temple (2 Thessalonians 2:4)
Is God (John 1:1-2; 10:36)	Claims to be God (2 Thessalonians 2:4)
Is the Lion from Judah (Revelation 5:5)	Has a mouth like a lion (Revelation 13:2)
Makes a peace covenant with Israel (Ezekiel 37:26)	Makes a peace covenant with Israel (Daniel 9:27)
Followers sealed on their forehead (Revelation 7:4; 14:1)	Followers sealed on their forehead or right hand (Revelation 13:16-18)
Crowned with many crowns (Revelation 19:12)	Crowned with ten crowns (Revelation 13:1)
Is the King of kings (Revelation 19:16)	Is called "the king" (Daniel 11:36)
Sits on a throne (Revelation 3:21; 12:5; 20:11)	Sits on a throne (Revelation 13:2; 16:10)
Rides a white horse (Revelation 19:11)	Rides a white horse (Revelation 6:2)
Has an army (Revelation 19:14)	Has an army (Revelation 19:19)
Violent death (Revelation 5:6; 13:8)	Violent death (Revelation 13:3)
Resurrection (Matthew 28:6)	Apparent resurrection (Revelation 13:3,14)
Thousand-year worldwide kingdom (Revelation 20:1-6)	Three-and-a-half-year worldwide kingdom (Revelation 13:5-8)

We can also observe notable *dissimilarities* between the antichrist and the true Christ:

- Foundationally, one is "the Christ" (Matthew 16:16); the other is "the antichrist" (1 John 4:3).

- One is a man of sorrows (Isaiah 53:3); the other the man of sin (2 Thessalonians 2:3).

- One is the Son of God (John 1:34); the other the son of perdition (2 Thessalonians 2:3).

- One is the Lamb (Isaiah 53:7); the other the beast (Revelation 11:7).

- One is the Holy One (Mark 1:24); the other the wicked one (2 Thessalonians 2:8).

- Christ came to do the Father's will (John 6:38); the antichrist will do his own will (Daniel 11:36).

- Christ submitted Himself to God (John 5:30); the antichrist will defy God (2 Thessalonians 2:4).

- Christ humbled Himself (Philippians 2:8); the antichrist will exalt himself (Daniel 11:37).

- Christ cleansed the temple (John 2:14,16); the antichrist will defile the temple (Matthew 24:15).

- Many human beings reject Christ (Isaiah 53:7); the antichrist will force masses of human beings to accept him (Revelation 13:4).

- Christ was a slain sacrifice for the people (John 11:51); the antichrist will be the slayer of people (Isaiah 14:20).

- Christ ascended into heaven (Luke 24:51); the antichrist will descend into the lake of fire (Revelation 19:20).

Jesus, the true Christ and holy Lamb, will defeat the beastly antichrist at His second coming (Revelation 19:11-16).

The False Prophet

Revelation 13:13-15 pictures the false prophet as a second beast and describes his work this way:

> He did astounding miracles, even making fire flash down to earth from the sky while everyone was watching. And with all the miracles he was allowed to perform on behalf of the first beast, he deceived all the people who belong to this world. He ordered the people to make a great statue of the first beast...He was then permitted to give life to this statue so that it could speak. Then the statue of the beast commanded that anyone refusing to worship it must die.

Satan does not have the power to engage in the grade-A miracles God does. However, he can perform lesser, grade-B miracles, and he empowers the false prophet to engage in these (see Exodus 7:11; 2 Timothy 3:8). The false prophet's goal with these miracles is to induce people to worship Satan's substitute for Christ—the antichrist (see Daniel 9:27; 11:31; 12:11; Matthew 24:15).

One of the miraculous acts the false prophet accomplishes is animating an image of the antichrist in the Jewish temple. The apostle Paul earlier revealed that the antichrist himself will sit in God's temple (see 2 Thessalonians 2:4) and demand the worship that rightly belongs only to God. When the antichrist is not present in the temple, an image of him is there to provide an object of worship in his absence (see Revelation 13:14-15; 14:9,11; 15:2; 16:2; 19:20; 20:4).

What is the significance of the false prophet giving breath to the image of the antichrist so that it appears to be alive and speaks? This apparent animation sets the image of the beast apart from typical idols in Old Testament times.[13] As we read in Psalm 135:15-16,

> The idols of the nations are merely things of silver
>   and gold,
>   shaped by human hands.
> They have mouths but cannot speak,
>   and eyes but cannot see.

They have ears but cannot hear,
> and mouths but cannot breathe.

Likewise, Habakkuk 2:19 says,

> "What sorrow awaits you who say to wooden idols,
>> 'Wake up and save us!'
> To speechless stone images you say,
>> 'Rise up and teach us!'
>> Can an idol tell you what to do?
> They may be overlaid with gold and silver,
>> but they are lifeless inside."

Contrary to such dead idols, this idolatrous image of the antichrist will seem to be alive, even godlike.

The false prophet will also control commerce on the earth by forcing everyone to receive the "mark of the beast." Only those who receive this mark can buy and sell during this time. As noted previously, this is a squeeze-play engineered to force people to worship the antichrist (Revelation 13:17).

The diabolical trinity—Satan, the antichrist, and the false prophet— will eventually experience total doom. In Revelation 19:20, we are told that the antichrist and the false prophet will be "thrown alive into the fiery lake of burning sulfur." This will take place after the tribulation period, before the beginning of Christ's millennial kingdom. Meanwhile, a mighty angel will cast Satan into "the bottomless pit" for the duration of Christ's millennial kingdom. After the millennial kingdom, Satan will be released from the bottomless pit and lead one last rebellion against God. God will promptly squash the rebellion and cast Satan into the lake of fire, where he will join the antichrist and false prophet. There they will be tormented day and night forever (Revelation 20:10).

Woe unto the entire cast of wicked characters of the end times. Eternal perdition. Endless suffering. Relentless ruin. Banished forever.

The Big Ideas

- *Gog* is the leader of a mighty end-times military coalition that will attack Israel. The coalition consists of Russia and Muslim nations.

- *Hardened sinners* will escalate explosively in the end times. They will be characterized by such things as humanism, materialism, and hedonism.

- *False messiahs, false prophets, and false teachers* will proliferate in the end times. Deception will run rampant.

- *The antichrist*, energized by Satan, will come into world dominion and demand worship as god. He will mimic Christ in many ways.

- *The false prophet*—the right-hand man of the antichrist—will seek to move the world to worship the antichrist.

Questions for Reflection

1. Do you think you could ever be deceived by false doctrine? Why or why not? (See Acts 17:11; 1 Thessalonians 5:21.)

2. How much time do you spend each week reading and meditating on the Word of God? What is your motivation for reading God's Word?

3. How much time do you spend daily in prayer?

4. What do you think of Martin Luther's comment: "I have so much to do that I shall spend the first three hours in prayer"?

8

Who Are the Spiritual Beings Behind the Scenes?

The late comedian Flip Wilson popularized the phrase, "The devil made me do it." Whenever he did something wrong or said something inappropriate, he'd say, "The devil made me do it." People laughed whenever he said it. Of course, such comedy routines subtly communicate that a personal devil operating behind the scenes is nothing but a fairy tale. It is all make-believe. It is something to laugh at.

In reality, there is a devil, just as there are demons and holy angels, all of whom operate behind the scenes in our world. The Father and the Holy Spirit also operate behind the scenes. We will see that each of these spiritual beings plays a critically important role in the unfolding drama of the end times.

Satan and Demons

Satan and his fallen angels (demons) are the invisible bad guys in the end times. Among their activities:

Demons will promote false doctrine in the end times. First Timothy 4:1 reveals: "The Holy Spirit tells us clearly that in the last times some will turn away from the true faith; they will follow deceptive spirits and teachings that come from demons." Who can doubt this is happening in the very day in which we live? Some cults and false religions originated in the teachings of a fallen angel.

Satan will energize the antichrist during the tribulation period. Second Thessalonians 2:9 reveals that the antichrist will operate according to "Satan's working" (ESV), or "through the activity of Satan" (AMP), or "in accordance with the work/activity of Satan" (EXB). Revelation 13:2

speaks of Satan as a dragon empowering the antichrist: "The dragon gave the beast his own power and throne and great authority."

Satan and demons will battle God's angels in the heavenly realm at the midpoint of the tribulation period. "Then there was war in heaven. Michael and his angels fought against the dragon and his angels. And the dragon lost the battle, and he and his angels were forced out of heaven. This great dragon—the ancient serpent called the devil, or Satan, the one deceiving the whole world—was thrown down to the earth with all his angels" (Revelation 12:7-9). I believe Satan will personally indwell the antichrist at this point. Soon after, the antichrist—motivated by the devil—will engage in cruel and wrathful persecution of the Jews and believers (see Revelation 12).

Demons will inflict horrible pain upon human beings during the tribulation period. These demons will be "given power to sting like scorpions" (Revelation 9:3). They will so torture people that people will "seek death but will not find it. They will long to die, but death will flee from them" (verses 5-6). These demons will submit to a high-ranking fallen angel whose "name in Hebrew is Abaddon, and in Greek, Apollyon—the Destroyer" (verse 11). Apollyon acts under Satan's authority, who is the highest-ranking fallen angel.

Satan and all fallen angels are destined for the lake of fire, which is a synonym for hell (see Revelation 20:10).

THE WORK OF SATAN AND DEMONS AMONG UNBELIEVERS	
Satan blinds the minds of unbelievers to the truth of the gospel.	2 Corinthians 4:4
Satan seeks to snatch the Word of God from the hearts of unbelievers when they hear it.	Luke 8:12
Demons, under Satan's lead, work to disperse false doctrine.	1 Timothy 4:1
Demons wield influence over false prophets.	1 John 4:1-4
Demons try to turn people to the worship of idols.	Leviticus 17:7; Deuteronomy 32:17; Psalm 106:36-38

God's Holy Angels

God's holy angels play a variety of roles in biblical prophecy. For example, God sometimes communicates prophecies to humans through angels. Recall that the Father gave "revelations" in the book of Revelation to Jesus, who then gave it to His angel. Christ's angel then passed these revelations on to John (Revelation 1:1-2).

In Luke 1:30-33, we read of an angel appearing to Mary to inform her of the prophetic future of her son:

> "Don't be afraid, Mary," the angel told her, "for you have found favor with God! You will conceive and give birth to a son, and you will name him Jesus. He will be very great and will be called the Son of the Most High. The Lord God will give him the throne of his ancestor David. And he will reign over Israel forever; his Kingdom will never end!"

The angel's prophetic words will find fulfillment when Christ reigns from the throne of David during the future thousand-year millennial kingdom (see 2 Samuel 7:12-14).

Angels also sometimes explain the meanings of prophecies to humans. In Daniel 10, we witness an angel explaining the future to Daniel. Daniel had not understood some of the end-time prophecies about his people. An angel soon appeared to Daniel and said, "Don't be afraid, Daniel. Since the first day you began to pray for understanding and to humble yourself before your God, your request has been heard in heaven. I have come in answer to your prayer" (Daniel 10:12). The angel then said, "Now I am here to explain what will happen to your people in the future, for this vision concerns a time yet to come" (verse 14).

Angels also play a role in announcing God's instructions and judgments throughout the tribulation period. We find an example of this in Revelation 14:6-11:

> And I saw another angel flying through the sky, carrying the eternal Good News to proclaim to the people who belong to this world—to every nation, tribe, language, and people. "Fear God," he shouted. "Give glory to him.

For the time has come when he will sit as judge. Worship him who made the heavens, the earth, the sea, and all the springs of water."

Then another angel followed him through the sky, shouting, "Babylon is fallen—that great city is fallen— because she made all the nations of the world drink the wine of her passionate immorality."

Then a third angel followed them, shouting, "Anyone who worships the beast and his statue or who accepts his mark on the forehead or on the hand must drink the wine of God's anger. It has been poured full strength into God's cup of wrath. And they will be tormented with fire and burning sulfur in the presence of the holy angels and the Lamb. The smoke of their torment will rise forever and ever, and they will have no relief day or night, for they have worshiped the beast and his statue and have accepted the mark of his name."

At the very end of the tribulation period, the angels will make still another announcement of judgment. The apostle John describes this for us:

Then I saw an angel standing in the sun, shouting to the vultures flying high in the sky: "Come! Gather together for the great banquet God has prepared. Come and eat the flesh of kings, generals, and strong warriors; of horses and their riders; and of all humanity, both free and slave, small and great" (Revelation 19:17-18).

The angels not only announce God's judgments, but they also execute some of them. We read in Revelation 16:1, "Then I heard a mighty voice from the Temple say to the seven angels, 'Go your ways and pour out on the earth the seven bowls containing God's wrath.'" These angel-inflicted judgments will cause such horrors as painful sores, death, unbearably intense heat from the sun, darkness over the land, and a violent earthquake (see Revelation 16:2-18). The tribulation will genuinely be a frightening time to be living on this planet.

Perhaps the most glorious role of angels in the end times involves their accompanying Christ at the second coming: "When the Son of Man comes in his glory, and all the angels with him, then he will sit upon his glorious throne" (Matthew 25:31). Revelation 19:14 affirms that when Christ comes again, "the armies of heaven, dressed in the finest of pure white linen, followed him on white horses." Notice the reference to "armies" (plural). Many Bible expositors believe that one army refers to the redeemed Christians who were raptured before the tribulation period. The other army is angelic. It will be an incredible spectacle.

Following the second coming, Christ's angels will gather the wicked and cast them into eternal fire. In His parable of the weeds, Jesus speaks about sowing good seed in a field, pulling up weeds and burning them, and bringing in the harvest. In Matthew 13:37-43, He explains the symbolism of this parable:

> Jesus replied, "The Son of Man is the farmer who plants the good seed. The field is the world, and the good seed represents the people of the Kingdom. The weeds are the people who belong to the evil one. The enemy who planted the weeds among the wheat is the devil. The harvest is the end of the world, and the harvesters are the angels.
>
> "Just as the weeds are sorted out and burned in the fire, so it will be at the end of the world. The Son of Man will send his angels, and they will remove from his Kingdom everything that causes sin and all who do evil. And the angels will throw them into the fiery furnace, where there will be weeping and gnashing of teeth. Then the righteous will shine like the sun in their Father's Kingdom. Anyone with ears to hear should listen and understand!"

As for the destiny of the holy angels, they will live with believers in the eternal city, the New Jerusalem (Revelation 21). Presented to our amazed gaze in Revelation 21 is a scene of such transcendent splendor that the human mind can scarcely take it in. This is a scene of ecstatic joy and fellowship of sinless angels and redeemed glorified human beings. The voice of the One identified as the Alpha and the Omega, the beginning and the end, will utter a climactic declaration: "Look, I am making everything new!" (Revelation 21:5).

Once believers are with the angels in this heavenly city, believers will apparently be in authority over the angels. The apostle Paul made this point to the Corinthian believers: "Don't you realize that we will judge angels?" (1 Corinthians 6:3).

TYPES OF ANGELS IN THE BIBLE		
Type of Angel	Ministry	Scripture
Michael the archangel	Ruling angel	Daniel 10:13; Jude 9
Cherubim	High-ranking guardians	Ezekiel 1:1-18
Seraphim	"Burning Ones," afire with adoration of God	Isaiah 6:1-7
Gabriel	Mighty one of God	Daniel 9:21; Luke 1:19
Watchers	God's reconnaissance agents on earth	Daniel 4:13

The Father

God the Father—the first person of the Trinity—knows the end from the beginning. His ability to foretell future events separates Him from all the false gods of paganism. The book of Isaiah makes the case convincingly. Addressing the polytheism of Isaiah's time, God Himself affirmed in no uncertain terms that because He alone can reveal the future, there is no other true God. Indeed, God says, "There is no other Rock—not one" (Isaiah 44:11); "There is no other God but me" (45:21); "I alone am God! I am God, and there is none like me. Only I can tell you the future before it even happens" (46:9-10).

Anyone can make predictions—that is easy. But having them fulfilled is another story altogether. The more statements you make about the future and the greater the detail, the better the chances that you will be proven wrong. But God the Father has never been wrong. This is borne out in the over one hundred precise messianic prophecies in the Old Testament pointing to the first coming of Jesus Christ (see, for example, Genesis 3:15; 12:3; 49:10; Psalm 2:7-9; 16:9-10; Jeremiah 23:5-6; Isaiah 7:14; 40:3; 53; Micah 5:2; Zechariah 9:9; 12:10; Daniel 9:24-25). Why did the Father get them all right? Because He knows the future just as clearly as He knows the past.

This relates to the Father's omniscience. Scripture reveals that God knows *all* things (Isaiah 41:22; 46:9-11; Matthew 11:21-23; Hebrews 4:13). The Father's knowledge is *infinite* (Psalm 33:13-15; 139:11-12; Proverbs 15:3; Isaiah 40:14; Acts 15:17-18; 1 John 3:20).

The Bible book that tells us more about end-times prophecy than any other book is Revelation. The prophetic "revelations" in this book passed from the *Father* to *Jesus* to *Jesus's angel* to *John*: "This is a revelation from Jesus Christ, which God [the Father] gave him to show his servants the events that must soon take place. He sent an angel to present this revelation to his servant John" (Revelation 1:1).

God the Father blesses the one who studies end-times prophecy and obeys its message: "God blesses the one who reads the words of this prophecy to the church, and he blesses all who listen to its message and obey what it says, for the time is near" (Revelation 1:3).

The Father will also be involved in specific events that transpire during the tribulation period. When the antichrist executes God's two prophetic witnesses at the midpoint of the tribulation period, we read that "after three and a half days, God breathed life into them, and they stood up" (Revelation 11:11). The Father will resurrect them from the dead, and they will ascend into heaven.

Meanwhile, God the Father will providentially protect the Jewish remnant during the second half of the tribulation period (Revelation 12:6). He will guard them against the forces of the antichrist.

Not unexpectedly, God the Father will be the ongoing target of the antichrist's blasphemies during the tribulation period (Revelation 13:1,5,6). Unbelievers will also curse the name of God repeatedly (16:9).

One day, you and I as Christians will dwell eternally in a heavenly city called the New Jerusalem. It is the City of God the Father (Revelation 3:12; 21:2). God will live among us (21:3,7). Scripture reveals that "the city has no need of sun or moon, for the glory of God illuminates the city" (21:23). We will sing praises to Him:

> "You are worthy, O Lord our God,
>> to receive glory and honor and power.
> For you created all things,
>> and they exist because you created what you pleased."
>>>>> (Revelation 4:11)

The angels, too, will worship the Father "with their faces to the ground" (7:11; see also 11:16).

How awesome is the Father!

The Holy Spirit

The Holy Spirit also plays a major role in biblical prophecy. Foundationally, the Holy Spirit inspired Scripture (2 Timothy 3:15-16). The work of the Holy Spirit (the "spirit of truth"—John 16:13) guarantees that the Bible is "the word of truth" (2 Timothy 2:15). You can trust Bible prophecy because of the work of the Holy Spirit in inspiring Scripture.

Second Peter 1:21 provides a critical insight regarding the human-divine interchange in the inspiration of Scripture. This verse informs us that "no prophecy in Scripture ever came from the prophet's own understanding, or from human initiative. No, those prophets were moved by the Holy Spirit, and they spoke from God."

The Greek phrase translated *moved* in this verse means "forcefully borne along." Even though humans were the writers of Scripture, they were all "borne along" by the Holy Spirit. The human wills of the authors were not the originators of God's message. God did not permit the will of sinful human beings to misdirect or erroneously record His message. Put another way, the Holy Spirit *moved* and the prophet *mouthed* these revelational truths. The Holy Spirit *revealed* and man *recorded* His Word to humankind.

INERRANCY OF SCRIPTURE (TRUSTWORTHINESS OF PROPHECY)	
All God's words are true.	Psalm 119:160
Smallest details are accurate.	Matthew 5:17-18
Every word of God is flawless.	Psalm 12:6; 18:30; Proverbs 30:5-6
God's commands are true.	Psalm 119:151
God's Word is truth.	John 17:17
Law of the Lord is perfect.	Psalm 19:7
Letters of words are accurate.	Matthew 22:41-46
Ordinances of the Lord are sure.	Psalm 19:9
Scripture cannot be broken.	John 10:35
Singular word is accurate.	Galatians 3:16
Words come from God.	Matthew 4:4

Apart from the inspiration of Scripture, the Holy Spirit plays a key role in restraining the emergence of the antichrist up till the time of the rapture. In 2 Thessalonians 2:5-8, the apostle Paul tells us:

> Don't you remember that I told you about all this when I was with you? And you know what is holding him [the antichrist] back, for he can be revealed only when his time comes. For this lawlessness is already at work secretly, and it will remain secret until the one who is holding it back [the Holy Spirit] steps out of the way. Then the man of lawlessness [the antichrist] will be revealed (inserts added for clarification).

I believe there is solid scriptural evidence that the one who is holding back the antichrist is the Holy Spirit, and he "steps out of the way" at the rapture. Here is the theological backdrop:

When the rapture occurs, the church—the universal body of believers in Christ (Ephesians 1:3; 2:5; see also Acts 1:5; 1 Corinthians

12:13)—will be raptured or caught up to be with Christ in the air. We know the Holy Spirit indwells the church because 1 Corinthians 3:16 tells us, "Don't you realize that all of you together are the temple of God and that the Spirit of God lives in you?" First Corinthians 6:19 likewise tells us, "Don't you realize that your body is the temple of the Holy Spirit, who lives in you and was given to you by God?" So, when the Holy Spirit–indwelt church meets Christ in the air at the rapture (John 14:1-3; 1 Corinthians 15:51-54; 1 Thessalonians 4:13-17), the Holy Spirit "steps out of the way" to allow for the emergence of the antichrist, as energized by Satan (2 Thessalonians 2:9). Put another way, while the Holy Spirit *steps out of the way*, Satan *steps up* and initiates the manifestation of his man of lawlessness—the antichrist.

I want to be careful not to miscommunicate here. When Scripture affirms that the Holy Spirit "steps out of the way," this means He will no longer be restraining the emergence of the antichrist. But He *will* continue His important work on earth in bringing people to salvation. Prophetic Scripture reveals that a multitude of people will become believers in Jesus during the tribulation period:

> After this I saw a vast crowd, too great to count, from every nation and tribe and people and language, standing in front of the throne and before the Lamb. They were clothed in white robes and held palm branches in their hands. And they were shouting with a great roar, "Salvation comes from our God who sits on the throne and from the Lamb!" (Revelation 7:9-14).

Such massive conversions to Christ would be impossible apart from the saving work of the Holy Spirit (see John 15:26; 16:8-11; 1 Corinthians 2:9–3:2; Ephesians 4:30; Titus 3:5). These countless conversions during the darkest period of human history virtually shout the grace of God.

Once the tribulation period is over, and Christ establishes His millennial kingdom, there will be great spiritual blessings all over the earth because of the work of the Holy Spirit. He will be present with—*and indwell*—all believers:

- "I will pour out my Spirit on your descendants, and my blessing on your children" (Isaiah 44:3).

- "I will put my Spirit in you so that you will follow my decrees and be careful to obey my regulations" (Ezekiel 36:27).

- "I will put my Spirit in you, and you will live again and return home to your own land. Then you will know that I, the LORD, have spoken, and I have done what I said. Yes, the LORD has spoken!" (Ezekiel 37:14).

- "I will pour out my Spirit upon all people. Your sons and daughters will prophesy. Your old men will dream dreams, and your young men will see visions. In those days I will pour out my Spirit even on servants—men and women alike" (Joel 2:28-29).

How awesome it will be. Praise You, Holy Spirit!

The Big Ideas

- A variety of spiritual beings play major roles in the unfolding drama of the end times.

- Satan will energize the antichrist.

- Demons will promote false doctrine and inflict torture on human beings during the tribulation period.

- God's holy angels will battle Satan and the fallen angels, announce God's judgments during the tribulation period, execute many of God's judgments, accompany Christ at the second coming, and gather the wicked for judgment.

- The Father is the ultimate source of prophecy. He will be involved in many specific events that unfold during the tribulation period. Eventually, Christians will live face-to-face with the Father in the New Jerusalem.

- The Holy Spirit inspired Scripture, including prophetic

Scripture. He will step out of the way at the rapture, thus enabling the emergence of the antichrist. He will bring about many conversions to Christ during the tribulation period, and He will bring immeasurable spiritual blessing during the millennial kingdom.

Questions for Reflection

1. What does it mean to you personally that God the Father "blesses the one who reads the words of this prophecy to the church, and he blesses all who listen to its message and obey what it says, for the time is near" (Revelation 1:3)?

2. Do you think an angel behind the scenes has ever ministered to you personally?

3. We need not wait till we are in heaven to praise God with the words from Revelation 4:11. *Why not praise God right now?* "You are worthy, O Lord our God, to receive glory and honor and power. For you created all things, and they exist because you created what you pleased."

9

Who Are the Good Guys?

We are beginning to see that the unfolding drama of the end
times involves quite a cast of characters. We explored the iden-
tities of the bad guys in chapter 7. We focused on spirit beings who
operate behind the scenes in chapter 8. In the present chapter, we'll
complete our exploration of the prophetic cast of characters, narrow-
ing our attention to the good guys. These include Jesus Christ, the
144,000 Jewish evangelists, God's two prophetic witnesses, the great
multitude of believers, the redeemed Jewish remnant (Israel), and the
"sheep" and "brothers" mentioned at Christ's judgment of the nations.
We begin our exploration with the Person who is the heart and center
of Bible prophecy—Jesus Christ.

Jesus Christ

Foundationally, Jesus is the revealer of the prophetic future. We've
already seen that He delivered the Father's revelations about the end
times to John: "This is a revelation *from Jesus Christ*, which God gave
him to show his servants the events that must soon take place. He sent
an angel to present this revelation to his servant John" (Revelation 1:1).

Jesus often spoke prophetically to His followers. In the upper room,
for example, Jesus affirmed He would one day come for His followers
at the rapture and bring them back with Him to heaven. Meanwhile,
He is busy preparing a place for them in heaven (John 14:1-3; see also
Revelation 21). Following the rapture, Jesus will preside over the judgment of Christians in heaven (2 Corinthians 5:10).

During the tribulation period, which follows sometime after the rapture, Jesus will inflict judgments upon the wicked on earth (Revelation 6). Each time Christ opens a seal from the divine scroll, a new judgment unfolds on humankind.

Jesus preached a prophetic sermon known as the Olivet Discourse, so named because He was sitting on the Mount of Olives when He delivered it (Matthew 24–25). The disciples had come to Him to inquire, "Tell us, when will all this happen? What sign will signal your return and the end of the world?" (24:3). We should view the entire Olivet Discourse as His response to this question.

Highlights of Jesus's teaching in this discourse include His prediction of the signs of the end of the age—such as the appearance of false Christs, wars, earthquakes, famines, the desecration of the Jewish temple, various cosmic disturbances, and the sign of His coming (Matthew 24:4-31). He also spoke of how the end times will be much like the days of Noah:

> "In those days before the flood, the people were enjoying banquets and parties and weddings right up to the time Noah entered his boat. People didn't realize what was going to happen until the flood came and swept them all away. That is the way it will be when the Son of Man comes" (Matthew 24:38-39).

In the Olivet Discourse, Jesus consistently stressed the importance of being ready for when He returns (Matthew 24:32-35,45-51; 25:1-13,14-30). He also prophesied about the judgment of the nations that will transpire immediately following His second coming (25:31-46). This judgment will determine who may enter Christ's thousand-year millennial kingdom (see Revelation 20:2-5). Christ Himself will be the judge.

I find it fascinating that Christ also spoke through the Old Testament prophets (see 1 Peter 1:10-11). Hence, when Daniel spoke about the revived Roman Empire headed by the antichrist (Daniel 2; 7), and when Zechariah spoke of Christ ascending the Mount of Olives following His second coming (Zechariah 14:4), and when Isaiah spoke about the millennial kingdom (Isaiah 2:2-4,9-21; 11:1-2; 24:1-13,16-23; 26:20-21; 35:1-10), it was the Spirit of Christ that spoke through all of them. Christ truly is the revealer of prophecy.

CHRIST: THE HEART AND CENTER OF PROPHECY	
Comes for Christians at the rapture	John 14:1-3; 1 Thessalonians 4:13-17
Presides at the judgment seat of Christ (a judgment of Christians)	2 Corinthians 5:10
Inflicts tribulation judgments	Revelation 6
Returns at the second coming	Revelation 19:11-21
Presides at the judgment of the nations	Matthew 25:31-46
Reigns in the millennial kingdom	2 Samuel 7:12-13; Luke 1:32
Presides over the great white throne judgment	Revelation 20:11-15

Because Jesus is the heart and center of Bible prophecy, it is understandable that much prophecy also relates to the followers of Jesus. For example, Scripture reveals that Satan will persecute all who "maintain their testimony for Jesus" during the tribulation period (Revelation 12:17; 14:12). Many of Jesus's servants will experience martyrdom during this time (Revelation 6:11; 17:6). Those who suffer martyrdom for their "testimony about Jesus" will come to life again and will rule with Christ during His millennial kingdom (Revelation 20:4).

At the end of the millennial kingdom, the wicked dead of all time will face Christ at the great white throne judgment (Revelation 20:11-14). Christ will judge them based on their evil deeds. Following this, Christ will cast them into the lake of fire (20:15).

Christ will then reign forever and ever (Revelation 11:15) and dwell directly with believers in the New Jerusalem (21).

Jesus plays such a major role in the end times that I wrote a book titled *Jesus and the End Times: What He Said...and What the Future Holds* (Harvest House Publishers, 2019). You may wish to add it to your reading list.

The 144,000 Jewish Witnesses

In Revelation 7:4, we read: "I heard how many were marked with the seal of God—144,000 were sealed from all the tribes of Israel." Some modern Christians have taken this as a metaphorical reference to the church. However, the context shows the verse is referring to 144,000 Jewish men—12,000 from each tribe—who minister during the first half of the tribulation period (see Revelation 14:4).

The mention of specific tribes in this context—along with specific numbers for each of those twelve tribes—removes all possibility that this is a figure of speech. Nowhere else in the Bible does a reference to twelve tribes of Israel mean anything but twelve tribes of Israel. The word "tribe" *always* refers to a literal ethnic group in Scripture.

The backdrop to a proper understanding of the 144,000 during the tribulation is that God initially chose the Jews to be His witnesses. Their appointed task was to share the good news of God with all other people around the world (see Isaiah 42:6; 43:10). The Jews were to be God's representatives to the Gentile peoples. The Jews failed at this task, especially since they did not even recognize Jesus as the divine Messiah.

During the future tribulation period, these 144,000 Jews will become believers in Jesus, the divine Messiah. And they will finally fulfill this mandate from God as His witnesses all around the world.

God will protectively "seal" these Jewish witnesses who become believers in Jesus. Seals in Bible times were signs of ownership and protection. These Jewish believers will be "owned" by God, and by His sovereign authority He will protect them during their time of service in the tribulation period (Revelation 14:1-4; see also 13:16-18; 2 Corinthians 1:22; Ephesians 1:13; 4:30).

These sealed servants of God will apparently be preachers. They will fulfill Matthew 24:14: "The Good News about the Kingdom will be preached throughout the whole world, so that all nations will hear it; and then the end will come."

These Jews likely become believers in Jesus in a way similar to that of the apostle Paul, himself a Jew (see Acts 9:1-9). Interestingly, in 1 Corinthians 15:8, Paul spoke of his conversion to Christ "as though I had been born at the wrong time." Some Bible expositors believe Paul may have been alluding to his 144,000 Jewish tribulation brethren, who would be spiritually born in a way similar to his spiritual birth—only Paul was spiritually born long before they were.

THE 144,000 JEWISH EVANGELISTS	
There will be 144,000 Jewish evangelists.	Revelation 7, 14
They will be honest and blameless.	Revelation 14:5
The Lamb's and Father's names will be on their foreheads.	Revelation 14:1
They will learn a new song.	Revelation 14:3
They will live in purity.	Revelation 14:4
They are among the redeemed.	Revelation 14:3
They are sealed from every tribe.	Revelation 7:4

God's Two Mighty Prophets

During the tribulation period, God will raise up two mighty witnesses who will testify to the true God with astounding power for half the tribulation period (1260 days). The miraculous power of these witnesses brings to mind Elijah (1 Kings 17; Malachi 4:5) and Moses (Exodus 7–11). Significantly, Old Testament law required two witnesses to confirm testimony (see Deuteronomy 17:6; 19:15; Matthew 18:16; John 8:17; Hebrews 10:28). In Revelation 11:3,5-6, we read God's prophetic promise:

"I will give power to my two witnesses, and they will be clothed in burlap and will prophesy during those 1,260 days."

...If anyone tries to harm them, fire flashes from their mouths and consumes their enemies. This is how anyone who tries to harm them must die. They have power to shut the sky so that no rain will fall for as long as they prophesy. And they have the power to turn the rivers and oceans into blood, and to strike the earth with every kind of plague as often as they wish.

Many expositors believe the two witnesses are not just *similar* to Moses and Elijah, but will actually *be* Moses and Elijah. Among their reasons:

1. The tribulation is the seventieth week of Daniel (Daniel 9:26-27). This will be a period in which God deals with the Jews—just as He did in the first sixty-nine weeks of Daniel. Moses and Elijah are unquestionably the two most influential figures in Jewish history. It would thus make good sense that they are on the scene during the tribulation period.

2. Moses and Elijah appeared on the mount of transfiguration with Jesus. This shows their importance and their centrality in God's purposes.

3. The miracles portrayed in Revelation 11 are very similar to those previously performed by Moses and Elijah in Old Testament times.

4. Both the Old Testament and Jewish tradition expected Moses (Deuteronomy 18:15,18) and Elijah (Malachi 4:5) to return in the end times.

While these reasons are valid and may yield a correct conclusion, we cannot be dogmatic. Two entirely new prophets of God may come on the scene during the tribulation period.

The time frame of these two witnesses—1260 days—measures out to precisely three-and-one-half years. It is not clear from Revelation 11 whether this is the first or the last three-and-one-half years of the tribulation.

It may be best to conclude that they do their miraculous work during the first three-and-one-half years. The antichrist's execution of them seems to fit best with other events that will transpire at the midpoint of the tribulation—such as the antichrist's exaltation of himself to godhood. The resurrection of the two witnesses—after being dead for three days—would make a more significant impact on the world at the midpoint of the tribulation than at the end, just before the second coming of Christ.

Revelation 11:8-12 describes their execution:

> Their bodies will lie in the main street of Jerusalem, the city that is figuratively called "Sodom" and "Egypt," the city where their Lord was crucified. And for three and a half days, all peoples, tribes, languages, and nations will stare at their bodies. No one will be allowed to bury them. All the people who belong to this world will gloat over them and give presents to each other to celebrate the death of the two prophets who had tormented them.
>
> But after three and a half days, God breathed life into them, and they stood up! Terror struck all who were staring at them. Then a loud voice from heaven called to the two prophets, "Come up here!" And they rose to heaven in a cloud as their enemies watched.

This resurrection will serve as a powerful testimony to the power of God during the tribulation. How awesome a day this will be. In my mind's eye, I can picture the two prophets being raised from the dead, and then asking the shocked onlookers: "Any questions?"

GOD'S TWO PROPHETIC WITNESSES	
They will prophesy 1260 days.	Revelation 11:3
Fire will consume any who try to kill them.	Revelation 11:5
They will have miraculous powers.	Revelation 11:6
The antichrist will put them to death.	Revelation 11:7
Their dead bodies will lie in the street.	Revelation 11:8
People worldwide will celebrate their deaths.	Revelation 11:9-10
They will resurrect from the dead.	Revelation 11:11
They will ascend into heaven.	Revelation 11:12
One brings to mind Elijah.	1 Kings 17; Malachi 4:5
The other brings to mind Moses.	Exodus 7, 11

The Great Multitude of Believers

In Revelation 7:9-10, we read: "After this I saw a vast crowd, too great to count, from every nation and tribe and people and language, standing in front of the throne and before the Lamb. They were clothed in white robes and held palm branches in their hands. And they were shouting with a great roar, 'Salvation comes from our God who sits on the throne and from the Lamb!'"

This passage reveals that a multitude of people will become believers during the tribulation period (see Matthew 25:31-46). Many may become convinced of the truth about salvation in Christ after witnessing millions of Christians supernaturally vanish off the planet at the rapture. Bibles and Christian books will probably still be around to explain the event. As well, many will no doubt become believers as a result of the ministry of the 144,000 Jewish evangelists introduced in Revelation 7. And many may become believers because of the miraculous ministry of God's two mighty prophets introduced in Revelation 11.

Matthew 24:14 tells us that during the tribulation period, "the

Good News about the Kingdom will be preached throughout the whole world, so that all nations will hear it." Even though persecution and affliction will be widespread, and even though many will have hearts hardened against God, God in His mercy will have His witnesses on earth who spread His message about Jesus and the coming kingdom.

The book of Revelation portrays this vast multitude of believers as "standing in front of the throne and before the Lamb" (Revelation 7:9). This means they are now in heaven. They will have either died or experienced martyrdom during the tribulation. Such martyrdom is not unexpected, for in His Olivet Discourse Jesus warned that the tribulation period would involve "greater anguish than at any time since the world began. And it will never be so great again" (Matthew 24:21).

This multitude of believers will comprise many ethnic groups from around the world. God's love knows no boundaries. People from every nation will come to know the Lord in that day (Revelation 5:9).

These redeemed people will be "clothed in white robes" (Revelation 7:9). Revelation 3:5,18 reveals that white robes are the garments of overcoming believers. These white garments point to their righteous triumph (6:11; 7:13; 19:8,14).

Scripture reveals they will have "palm branches in their hands" (Revelation 7:9). Palm branches in Bible times were associated with celebrations (see John 12:13). This great multitude will have reason to celebrate, for their suffering is now over, and they will now enjoy the very presence of God. Never again will they be subject to persecution or death. In the presence of God are eternal pleasures (Psalm 16:11).

This great crowd will shout with a great roar, "Salvation comes from our God who sits on the throne and from the Lamb!" (Revelation 7:10). All who are present recognize that this awesome salvation comes from God on the throne and the Lamb of God, Jesus Christ. Though these believers experienced sorrow and suffering on earth, they are now joyful in heaven, loudly singing praises to the Father and the Lamb. Their worship is exuberant and unrestrained.

The Redeemed Remnant of Israel

At the midpoint of the tribulation period, the antichrist will break the covenant he earlier made with Israel. He will set up an image of himself within the Jewish temple in Jerusalem and demand worship (Revelation 13:13-15). In view of this coming desecration of the temple, Jesus issued the sternest of warnings to the Jews who will live in Jerusalem at this time:

> "Those in Judea must flee to the hills. A person out on the deck of a roof must not go down into the house to pack. A person out in the field must not return even to get a coat. How terrible it will be for pregnant women and for nursing mothers in those days. And pray that your flight will not be in winter or on the Sabbath. For there will be greater anguish than at any time since the world began. And it will never be so great again" (Matthew 24:16-21).

Jesus here instructs the Jews living in Jerusalem at this time to *run for their lives.* He tells them to not even pack their bags. The slightest delay in leaving could lead to death under the antichrist.

Upon escaping Jerusalem, this remnant of Jews will be supernaturally protected by God in the wilderness, perhaps in Bozrah or Petra, about eighty miles south of Jerusalem (Revelation 12:6,14). God will protect them for three-and-a-half years, the last half of the tribulation period.

At the very end of the tribulation period, however, the forces of the antichrist will move against this remnant of Israel. The Jews will sense impending doom as the forces of the antichrist gather in the rugged wilderness, poised to attack and annihilate them. From an earthly perspective, these Jews will be helpless, hopeless, and defenseless.

But then something wonderful will happen. God in His grace and mercy will remove the spiritual blindness that He inflicted upon the Jews following their rejection of Jesus as the promised Messiah (see Romans 9–11). Once their blindness has been removed, the Jews in the wilderness will promptly repent of their rejection of Jesus and believe in Him as their divine Messiah.

Hosea 6:1-3 shows that the Jewish leaders will call for the people of the nation to repent:

"Come, let us return to the LORD.
He has torn us to pieces;
   now he will heal us.
He has injured us;
   now he will bandage our wounds.
In just a short time he will restore us,
   so that we may live in his presence.
Oh, that we might know the LORD!
   Let us press on to know him.
He will respond to us as surely as the arrival of dawn
   or the coming of rains in early spring."

Whereas the Jewish leaders once led the Jewish people to reject Jesus as their Messiah, they will now urge repentance and instruct all to turn to Christ. This the remnant will do, and they will experience salvation.

In dire threat from the forces of the antichrist, the Jewish remnant will cry out to their newly found Messiah. They will plead for Him to return and deliver them (Zechariah 12:10; Matthew 23:37-39; see also Isaiah 53:1-9).

God will answer the prayers of the Jewish remnant (Romans 10:13-14). The divine Messiah will return personally to rescue His people from danger. The same Jesus who ascended into heaven will come again at the second coming (Acts 1:9-11).

Old Testament prophetic Scripture reveals that Jesus will return first to the mountain wilderness of Bozrah, where the Jewish remnant is in danger (Isaiah 34:1-7; 63:1-6; Micah 2:12-13; Habakkuk 3:3). *They will not be in danger for long!*

Christ will quickly defeat all who stand against the remnant of Israel. He will slay the antichrist. Habakkuk 3:13 prophesies of Christ's victory over the antichrist: "You went out to rescue your chosen people…You crushed the heads of the wicked and stripped their bones from head to toe." Likewise, in 2 Thessalonians 2:8, we read of the antichrist: "The Lord Jesus will slay him with the breath of his mouth and destroy him by the splendor of his coming."

The antichrist will be impotent and powerless in the face of the true

Christ. The divine Messiah will destroy all the forces of the antichrist from Bozrah all the way back to Jerusalem (Joel 3:12-13; Zechariah 14:12-15; Revelation 14:19-20).

What a wondrous day of deliverance that will be!

The "Sheep" and the "Brothers"

Immediately after His second coming to earth, Jesus will engage in the judgment of the nations. Jesus describes it for us in Matthew 25:31-46:

> "When the Son of Man comes in his glory, and all the angels with him, then he will sit on his glorious throne. Before him will be gathered all the nations, and he will separate people one from another as a shepherd separates the sheep from the goats. And he will place the sheep on his right, but the goats on the left. Then the King will say to those on his right, 'Come, you who are blessed by my Father, inherit the kingdom prepared for you from the foundation of the world. For I was hungry and you gave me food, I was thirsty and you gave me drink, I was a stranger and you welcomed me, I was naked and you clothed me, I was sick and you visited me, I was in prison and you came to me.' Then the righteous will answer him, saying, 'Lord, when did we see you hungry and feed you, or thirsty and give you drink? And when did we see you a stranger and welcome you, or naked and clothe you? And when did we see you sick or in prison and visit you?' And the King will answer them, 'Truly, I say to you, as you did it to one of the least of these my brothers, you did it to me.'
>
> "Then he will say to those on his left, 'Depart from me, you cursed, into the eternal fire prepared for the devil and his angels. For I was hungry and you gave me no food, I was thirsty and you gave me no drink, I was a stranger and you did not welcome me, naked and you did not clothe me, sick and in prison and you did not visit me.' Then they

also will answer, saying, 'Lord, when did we see you hungry or thirsty or a stranger or naked or sick or in prison, and did not minister to you?' Then he will answer them, saying, 'Truly, I say to you, as you did not do it to one of the least of these, you did not do it to me.' And these will go away into eternal punishment, but the righteous into eternal life.'" (ESV)

In this passage, we read about the good guys—the *sheep* and the *brothers*. But bad guys are also mentioned—the *goats*. Let's unpack what is going on here.

The nations mentioned in Matthew 25:31-46 are in two categorizes—the sheep and the goats, representing the saved and the lost among the Gentiles. According to Matthew 25:32, the intermingled Gentiles require separation by a special judgment. The basis of this judgment is how they treat Christ's "brothers" during the tribulation period.

Who are the brothers? I believe they are the 144,000 Jews mentioned in Revelation 7, Christ's Jewish brothers who bear witness of Him during the tribulation. These Jewish evangelists will find it difficult to buy food because they refused to receive the mark of the beast (Revelation 13:16-17). Only true believers in the Lord will jeopardize their lives by extending hospitality to these Jewish messengers. These sheep (believers) who treat the 144,000 brothers well will enter Christ's millennial kingdom. The goats—unbelievers who refused help to the 144,000—will go into eternal punishment.

Conclusion

Like all good dramas, the good guys win at the end of this divine redemption story. The bad guys get what is coming to them. This will become even clearer as we examine the WHAT, WHEN, WHERE, and WHY of Bible prophecy. In the next chapter, we will begin our discussion of the WHAT and WHEN. We will cover a great deal of ground, and *it will be fascinating!*

The Big Ideas

- Jesus is the heart of Bible prophecy. He will come for Christians at the rapture, judge Christians in heaven, inflict judgments during the tribulation, return at the second coming, judge the nations, set up the millennial kingdom, and preside over the great white throne judgment.

- The 144,000 Jewish evangelists will spread the gospel of the kingdom worldwide during the tribulation period.

- God's two mighty prophets will engage in miracles similar to those of Moses and Elijah, pointing to the one true God.

- A great multitude of believers will be the fruit of the labors of the 144,000 Jewish evangelists and God's two mighty prophets.

- The redeemed remnant of Jews will turn to Christ at the end of the tribulation period, after which Christ will return and rescue them from the forces of the antichrist.

- The "sheep" (saved Gentiles) will minister to the needs of Christ's "brothers" (the 144,000 Jews) during the tribulation. The sheep will be invited into Christ's millennial kingdom. The "goats" (unsaved Gentiles) will be excluded from the kingdom.

Questions for Reflection

1. Without looking back, can you remember five ways that Jesus is involved in end-times prophecy?

2. What do you think it says of God that during the darkest and most rebellious period of human history, He still gives opportunity for salvation to any who will listen? Allow the truth of God's relentless mercy to take root deep in your heart.

PART 3

WHAT ARE THE PRIMARY EVENTS OF THE END TIMES? *WHEN* DO THEY OCCUR?

10

Events Before the
Tribulation Period

I n our exploration of the WHO of Bible prophecy, we discovered there is a rich and varied cast of characters in the unfolding drama of the end times. We now turn our attention to the WHAT and WHEN of future prophetic events. In conjunction with the remaining vantage points—the WHERE and WHY—you will continue to gain a full, composite understanding of Bible prophecy.

To make it as easy as possible for you, I have spread about fifty prophetic events over five chapters, categorizing them into five chronological periods: events before the tribulation period, events in the first and second halves of the tribulation period, events at the end of (and right after) the tribulation period, events in the millennial kingdom, and events prior to and during the eternal state.

My explanations of the events will be brief and to the point. I will not overload you with details. My main concern in this book is to give you the big picture—an overview—of the primary prophetic events, and present them in the order I think they are most likely to occur. Later, if you are up to it, you are free to consult some of my other prophecy books for more comprehensive details.[14]

I know what you are likely thinking. Over fifty events seems like a lot. But don't fret. It is not complicated. I will be brief. It will all make good sense. Soon you will have a good grasp of end-times prophecy.

We begin in this chapter with an exploration of prophetic events that will unfold prior to the tribulation period, during the current church age.

God Continues to Unfold His Divine Plan for Both the Church and Israel

The church age began on the day of Pentecost (Acts 2; 11:15-16; 1 Corinthians 12:13) and will continue up till the time the church is raptured off the earth, before the tribulation period (1 Corinthians 15:50-58; 1 Thessalonians 4:13-17). During the church age, any who believe in Jesus become part of the church and will take part in the rapture. They will thereby escape the judgments that will fall on the world during the seven-year tribulation period (1 Thessalonians 1:10; Revelation 3:10).

God's purpose for Israel is more complicated because of the Jewish rejection of Christ in the first century. The Jews at that time wanted no part of Jesus or His kingdom offer. This resulted in a delay of the fulfillment of God's kingdom promises to Israel. These promises have now been postponed until Christ's millennial kingdom, which follows the second coming (see Matthew 11–12).

The Jewish rejection of Jesus carried severe divine consequences. Since the time of their rejection of Jesus in the first century, the Jews have experienced judicial blindness and hardening as a judgment from God (Romans 11:25). God will not lift this judicial blindness until the end of the tribulation period.

Meanwhile, God's goal is to make the Jews jealous for His offer of salvation. He has accomplished this by opening up the gospel to the Gentiles ever since the first century (Romans 11:11). With the Jews no longer in the special place of God's blessing, and with the Gentiles now experiencing God's salvation, God is slowly but surely moving the Jews toward repentance. At the end of the tribulation period, their blindness will finally be lifted, and the Jewish remnant will repent and turn to Jesus (11:25).

If that is God's plan for national Israel, then what about individual

Jews who place faith in Jesus during the current church age? Those Jews become a part of Christ's church (see Ephesians 3:3-5,9; Colossians 1:26-27) and will take part in the rapture.

Certain Characteristics Will Predominate During the Current Church Age

Jesus provided prophetic insights regarding the characteristics of the current church age in His parables in Matthew 13. These parables cover the period between Christ's two advents—His first and second comings.

The Parable of the Sower. In this parable, Jesus teaches that during the current age, the gospel seed will be sown onto different kinds of soil (Matthew 13:1-23). His meaning is that there will be various kinds of responses to the gospel since there will be different kinds of opposition to the gospel—including that from the world, the flesh, and the devil.

The Parable of the Weeds. In this parable, Jesus teaches that the sowing of the true gospel seed will be imitated by a false counter-sowing of "weeds" (Matthew 13:24–30). Only a judgment following the future tribulation period will separate the "wheat" (true believers) from the "weeds" (unbelievers or false believers).

The Parable of the Mustard Seed. In this parable, Jesus teaches that God's spiritual kingdom would have an almost imperceptible beginning—hardly even noticeable. But just as a small mustard seed can produce an enormous plant more than fifteen feet high, so God's spiritual kingdom would start small but grow to be exceptionally large in the world (Matthew 13:31-32).

The Parable of the Yeast. In this parable, Jesus seems to teach that false teaching may emerge and grow exponentially, even penetrating Christendom during the church age (Matthew 13:33-43). We certainly see false ideas about God, Jesus, and the gospel in the church today.

The Parable of the Hidden Treasure. In this parable, Jesus teaches about the incredible value of the true kingdom of heaven, as opposed to counterfeit belief systems. Those who genuinely see its importance will do anything within their power to possess it. They will allow nothing to stand in their way (Matthew 13:44).

The Parable of the Pearl. In this parable, Jesus likewise teaches about the great worth of the true kingdom of heaven, as opposed to counterfeit belief systems. Those who genuinely see its importance will do anything within their power to possess it (Matthew 13:45-46).

The Parable of the Fishing Net. Fishermen can attest that when a net comes up out of the water, it contains all kinds of fish—some of them good and worth keeping, but others that are useless. Fishermen always separate the good from the bad. In this parable, Jesus teaches that until His second coming, when judgment will take place, there will be both genuine Christians and phony (professing) Christians coexisting within the kingdom. At the end of the age, there will be a separation of the righteous from the unrighteous. Christ will invite the righteous (true believers) into His millennial kingdom. He will exclude the unrighteous (professing or phony believers) from His kingdom and send them to a place of suffering (Matthew 13:47-51).

Israel's Rebirth as a Nation

I previously noted that God still has a plan for the future of Israel (Romans 9–11). Ezekiel 36 and 37 prophesied that Israel would become a nation again after a long and worldwide dispersion. Against all odds, Israel's rebirth as a nation in 1948 was a direct fulfillment of biblical prophecies. Since then, just as prophesied, the Jews have been streaming back to the Holy Land from every nation in the world. The primary motivation of Jews relocating back to the Holy Land is worldwide anti-Semitism. All this is setting the stage for when the antichrist will sign a covenant with newly born Israel—an event that will begin the tribulation period (Daniel 9:27).

ISRAEL IN PROPHECY	
Israel was prophesied to be reborn in the latter days. Israel became a nation again in 1948.	Ezekiel 36–37
Israel will be a sore spot in the world in the end times.	Zechariah 12:2-3
Israel will be invaded by a northern military coalition in the end times.	Ezekiel 38–39
God will deliver Israel from the northern military coalition.	Ezekiel 39
The antichrist's covenant will bring temporary protection and security to Israel.	Daniel 9:27
The Jewish temple will be rebuilt during the tribulation period.	Matthew 24:1-2,15,27-31; Daniel 9:26-27; 11:31
The antichrist will break his covenant with Israel and make Jerusalem his throne.	Daniel 11:40-45
The antichrist will defile the Jewish temple.	2 Thessalonians 2:1-4
A Jewish remnant will escape Jerusalem.	Matthew 24:16-22
The Jewish remnant will trust in Jesus as Messiah.	Zechariah 12:2–13:1; Romans 11:25-27

Apostasy Will Escalate as We Near the End Times

Apostasy will escalate as never before in the end times. The apostle Paul tells us more about this than any other biblical writer. He affirms that "in the last times some will turn away from the true faith; they will follow deceptive spirits and teachings that come from demons" (1 Timothy 4:1). Moreover, "people will love only themselves and their money. They will be boastful and proud, scoffing at God, disobedient to their parents, and ungrateful." Paul says, "They will consider nothing sacred. They will be unloving and unforgiving; they will slander others and have no self-control. They will be cruel and hate what is good." He warns that "they will betray their friends, be reckless, be puffed up with pride, and love pleasure rather than God. They will act religious, but they will reject the power that could make them godly" (2 Timothy 3:1-5).

Along these same lines, Paul affirms that "a time is coming when people will no longer listen to sound and wholesome teaching. They will follow their own desires and will look for teachers who will tell them whatever their itching ears want to hear. They will reject the truth and chase after myths" (2 Timothy 4:3-4).

All this means that apostasy will rise to a fever pitch before and during the tribulation period (Matthew 24:9-12). Even today, we witness the rise of pervasive apostasy. An example is how some Christian leaders today say God is not all-powerful, God is not all-knowing, Jesus made mistakes when He was on earth, and Jesus is not the only way of salvation. Things will get even worse in the years to come.

The United States May Weaken as We Progress into the End Times

The United States of Europe—the revived Roman Empire led by the antichrist—will become a political and economic superpower during the first part of the tribulation period (see Daniel 2; 7). Scripture reveals that the antichrist will later shift his headquarters to Jerusalem at the midpoint of the tribulation period (Matthew 24:15-20; 2 Thessalonians 2:4), and then to commercial New Babylon, which will serve as his economic headquarters in the second half of the tribulation period (Revelation 18).

It seems logical to infer that for all this to happen, the United States may weaken in the end times, no longer the superpower it is today. This weakening could be due to a moral implosion, an economic collapse due to a national catastrophe, nuclear terrorism, an electromagnetic pulse (EMP) attack, or perhaps even the rapture—since so many Christians live in the United States. It is likely that the United States will eventually become an ally of the antichrist's global empire (Daniel 2; 7; Revelation 13).

The Rapture of the Church Is Imminent

The rapture is that glorious event in which the dead in Christ will be raised, living Christians will be instantly transformed into their glorified bodies, and both groups will meet Christ in the air and be taken back to heaven (John 14:1-3; 1 Corinthians 15:51-54; 1 Thessalonians 4:13-17). This will happen instantly. The bodies of both groups of believers will be imperishable, glorious, and powerful (1 Corinthians 15:42-43; 2 Corinthians 5:1-4).

The rapture will occur before the tribulation period. There are at least six scriptural factors that support this view:

1. No New Testament or Old Testament passage on the tribulation period mentions the church.

2. Jesus promised to keep the church from the "time of testing" coming upon "the whole world" (Revelation 3:10).

3. Jesus promised to deliver believers from the "the terrors of the coming judgment," or "the wrath to come" (ESV), in the tribulation period (1 Thessalonians 1:10).

4. God has not appointed the church to wrath (Romans 5:9; 1 Thessalonians 5:9). Since God's wrath will fall during the tribulation period, the church will not be there.

5. God typically delivers His people before His judgment falls (see 2 Peter 2:5-9).

6. Other Scriptures reveal that during the tribulation period God will deal specifically with the unbelieving nations (see Isaiah 26:21; Revelation 6:15-17) and with Israel (Jeremiah 30:7; Daniel 12:1-4), not the church.

We conclude that the rapture of the church is imminent. It could occur at any time.

As a Result of the Rapture, the Divine Restrainer—the Holy Spirit—Will No Longer Restrain the Antichrist

Second Thessalonians 2:6 affirms that the antichrist is presently being restrained. Only when the restrainer "steps out of the way" will the antichrist be able to reveal himself (verse 7). There is only one person—the omnipotent God—who is powerful enough to restrain Satan, who energizes the antichrist (2 Thessalonians 2:9; 1 John 4:4; Revelation 13:2).

I am convinced that the restrainer is the Holy Spirit, who indwells every believer in the church (1 Corinthians 3:16; 6:19). When Christ raptures the church from the earth before the tribulation, the restrainer (the Holy Spirit) *steps out of the way*. Satan concurrently *steps up* and energizes his lawless man—the antichrist.

The antichrist—also called "the beast" in Revelation 13:1—will rise to power in a revived Roman Empire (Daniel 2; 7). He will accomplish Satan's agenda throughout the tribulation period.

MEANWHILE IN HEAVEN

Following the Rapture, Christians Will Face the Judgment Seat of Christ in Heaven

It comes as a surprise to some Christians to learn that they will one day stand before the judgment seat of Christ (Romans 14:8-10; 1 Corinthians 3:11-15; 9:24-27). Christ will examine each believer's life regarding deeds done while on earth. He will also consider their motives and intents of the heart. This judgment has nothing to do with whether Christians will remain saved. Those who have placed faith in Christ are eternally secure, and nothing threatens that salvation (John 10:28-30; Romans 8:29-39; Ephesians 1:13; 4:30; Hebrews 7:25). This judgment rather has to do with the reception or loss of rewards for how one has lived on earth since becoming a Christian (1 Corinthians 3:12-15).

THE JUDGMENT OF CHRISTIANS	
Nature of	Scripture
Universal	"We will all stand before the judgment seat of God" (Romans 14:10).
Knowledge	The extent of one's knowledge of God's will is taken into consideration (Luke 12:48).
Works	"You repay all people according to what they have done" (Psalm 62:12).
Thoughts	"I am the one who searches out the thoughts and intentions of every person. And I will give to each of you whatever you deserve" (Revelation 2:23).
Words	"You must give an account on judgment day for every idle word you speak" (Matthew 12:36).
Salvation Is Secure	"If the work is burned up, the builder will suffer great loss. The builder will be saved, but like someone barely escaping through a wall of flames" (1 Corinthians 3:15).
Run the Race	Christians should seek to run the race well so they can obtain "the prize" (1 Corinthians 9:24-25).

The Marriage Between the Church and the Lamb Takes Place in Heaven

Jesus often referred to Himself as a bridegroom (Matthew 9:15; 22:2-14; 25:1-13; Mark 2:19-20; Luke 5:34-35; 14:15-24; John 3:29). The New Testament portrays the church as a virgin bride awaiting the coming of her heavenly Bridegroom (2 Corinthians 11:2). After the rapture—when the Groom comes for the Bride—the marriage of the Lamb will take place in heaven. Christ and the church will get "married." This will be the closest of spiritual unions. I can't even begin to imagine what it will be like.

BACK ON EARTH

Israel Will Live in Security and Be at Rest in Her Own Land

Scripture prophesies that in the end times, Israel will live in security and at rest in her own land (Ezekiel 38:11). I am convinced that even today, Israel is living in relative security and rest because of her powerful military, which can repel any attack from surrounding enemies. It is also possible that the Abraham Accords Peace Agreement, enacted in September 2020, contributes to this sense of security and rest.

Israel's state of security and rest is a precondition for the Ezekiel invasion (Ezekiel 38:1-11; see below). It is entirely possible that this invasion may take place sometime *after* the rapture but *before* the beginning of the tribulation period.

Keep in mind that the tribulation period does not begin immediately after the rapture. There may be some years between the rapture and the beginning of the tribulation period. The covenant the antichrist signs with Israel represents the actual beginning of the tribulation period (Daniel 9:27).

A Massive Northern Military Coalition Will Invade Israel

Despite any temporary Middle East peace accords that may exist, prophetic Scripture reveals that a massive northern military coalition will one day invade Israel. Scripture specifies the nations that will make up the invading force. These include Rosh (modern Russia), Magog (the former southern Soviet republics of Kazakhstan, Kyrgyzstan, Uzbekistan, Turkmenistan, Tajikistan), Meshech and Tubal (modern Turkey), Persia (the Islamic Republic of Iran), Ethiopia (modern Sudan), Put (modern Libya), and Gomer and Beth-Togarmah (both additional references to modern Turkey) (Ezekiel 38:1-6 NASB). Significantly, Russia has made alliances with many of these Muslim nations in our present day. The stage is being set for this invasion.

God Himself Will Destroy the Northern Military Coalition

God will utterly annihilate the northern invaders (Ezekiel 38:19-22). He will use five primary means to do so (Ezekiel 38:17–39:8).

First, God will cause a massive earthquake that will disrupt transportation and throw the armies of the multinational forces into chaos (Ezekiel 38:19-20).

Second, God will cause an outbreak of infighting among the invading troops (Ezekiel 38:21). He sovereignly induces the various armies of the invading forces to turn on and kill each other. This will be a friendly fire fiasco, all induced by God. Adding to the confusion is the fact that the armies of the various nations speak different languages—including Russian, Farsi, Arabic, and Turkic. Communication will be difficult. One realistic scenario is that the Muslim countries and Russia turn on each other, each suspecting a double-cross by the other.

Third, a massive outbreak of disease will kill large numbers of the various armies (Ezekiel 38:22a). Try to picture the scene: There has been an enormous earthquake, followed by heavy infighting among the invading troops. Countless dead bodies will be lying around everywhere. The earthquake will have disrupted transportation so it will be difficult if not impossible to transfer the wounded or bring in food and medicine. Meanwhile, myriad birds and other predatory animals will feast on this unburied flesh. All this is a recipe for the outbreak of pandemic disease which, according to Ezekiel, will take many lives.

Fourth, God will rain down torrential rain, hailstones, fire, and burning sulfur upon the invaders (Ezekiel 38:22b). It may be that the powerful earthquake sets off volcanic deposits in the region, thrusting into the atmosphere a hail of molten rock and burning sulfur (volcanic ash), which then falls upon the enemy troops, utterly destroying them.

Fifth, God will "rain down fire on Magog and on all your allies who live safely on the coasts" (Ezekiel 39:6). It may be that this judgment involves nuclear weaponry. God will destroy any possible Muslim strongholds that could pose a remaining threat to Israel.

The Stage Becomes Set for Further Prophecies to Unfold During the Tribulation Period

Try to picture this in your mind:

- The rapture of the church will have already taken place

before the tribulation period. This means there are no longer any true Christians on the earth, except for those who have converted since the beginning of the tribulation period.

- God has just destroyed the Muslim invaders.

- This means that the two most prominent religious groups—Christians and Muslims—that would no doubt resist the emergence of the false religious system associated with New Babylon (Revelation 17) are no longer around. This will make it much easier for the false religion to emerge.

- With Muslim countries neutralized by God's judgment, this also makes it much easier for the antichrist to catapult into world dominion. Keep in mind that the Muslims had intended to bring about a worldwide caliphate with Muslims in control. God has now removed that possibility, having destroyed the invading Muslim armies. This will make it easier for the antichrist to seize the moment and make his move onto the world stage.

- Still further, with Muslim resistance now at an all-time low because of God's judgment, the Jews will find it much easier to rebuild their temple. No longer will Israel feel a Muslim threat at rebuilding the temple.

In the next chapter, we will continue our investigation of the WHAT and WHEN of prophetic events related to the tribulation period.

The Big Issues

- Prophecy relates not only to the events of the tribulation period and beyond, but also to the course of the present age.

- The super-sign has already occurred: *Israel has been reborn as a nation.*

- What is taking place in our current age is setting the stage for the fulfillment of specific prophecies in the tribulation period.

- Things are unfolding in our world just as prophesied thousands of years ago.

Questions for Reflection

1. Knowing that the rapture could occur at any time, are you more motivated to walk in righteousness before the Lord? What changes might you want to make in your life?

2. How do you feel about the coming judgment seat of Christ, where Christians will be held accountable for how they lived? Is this a *concern* or a *comfort* to you?

3. What can you do to insulate yourself against the rising apostasy in our world?

11

Events in the First and Second Halves of the Tribulation

We began our investigation of the WHAT and WHEN of Bible prophecy in the previous chapter, exploring events prophesied to occur prior to the tribulation period. We continue in this chapter with a focus on events that will transpire during the first and second halves of the tribulation period.

To review, the tribulation period precisely lasts seven years. This divides into two equal periods of three-and-a-half years each. How do we know this? Foundationally, Daniel 9:27 equates the tribulation period with the "seventieth week of Daniel." This one "week" is seven years in length.

The book of Revelation corroborates this. Revelation 11:2 affirms that *half* the tribulation period is forty-two months (three-and-a-half years). Revelation 11:3 and 12:6 affirm that half the tribulation period is 1260 days (again, three-and-a-half years). Revelation 12:14 affirms that half the tribulation period is "a time, times, and half a time." "Time" is one year, "times" is two years, and "half a time" is half a year—totaling three-and-a-half years.

Here's the main thing to remember: *The tribulation period is seven years long, with the first and second halves each being three-and-a-half years in duration.*

SEVEN COMPONENTS OF THE TRIBULATION PERIOD
1. Scripture refers to a definite period of tribulation at the end of the age (Matthew 24:29-35).
2. It will be of such severity that no period in history past or future will equal it (Matthew 24:21).
3. It is called the time of Jacob's trouble, for it is a judgment on Messiah-rejecting Israel (Jeremiah 30:7; Daniel 12:1-4).
4. The Gentile nations will also be judged for their sin and rejection of Christ (Isaiah 26:21; Revelation 6:15-17).
5. This tribulation period lasts seven years (Daniel 9:24,27).
6. It will be purposefully limited to seven years (Matthew 24:22), for no flesh could survive it if it were longer.
7. It will be so bad that people will want to hide and even die (Revelation 6:16).

PROPHETIC EVENTS IN THE FIRST HALF OF THE TRIBULATION PERIOD

The Antichrist Will Sign a Covenant with Israel

Daniel 9:27 prophesies that the antichrist "shall make a strong covenant with many for one week, and for half of the week he shall put an end to sacrifice and offering" (ESV). The antichrist's signing of a covenant with Israel will mark the official beginning of the tribulation period.

Some Bible translations render the term *strong covenant* as a "firm covenant" (NASB) or a "binding and irrevocable covenant" (AMP). Apparently, the antichrist will solve the Middle East crisis and force all parties—Jewish and Muslim—to get along. It will be a strong covenant backed by the military might of the revived Roman Empire, over which the antichrist will rule. The idea is: *Obey the covenant or suffer the consequences.*

The Antichrist Will Rise Rapidly on the World Scene

The antichrist will start out in relative insignificance (Daniel 7:8,

20,21,24,25), but will escalate quickly on the world stage. He will become a highly impressive person. He will appear to be a genius in intellect (Daniel 8:23), commerce (Daniel 11:43; Revelation 13:16-17), war (Revelation 6:2; 13:2), speech (Daniel 11:36), and politics (Revelation 17:11-12). Satan—the unholy spirit—will energize him for his work (2 Thessalonians 2:9).

The antichrist will be ambitious to dominate the world. In the process, he will seek to destroy the Jews, persecute believers, and set up his own global anti-God kingdom (Revelation 13). He will even set himself up as god (2 Thessalonians 2:4). He will eventually become both the political and religious head of the world.

Early in the Tribulation Period, the Jews Will Rebuild Their Temple

The Jews will rebuild their temple during the first part of the tribulation period. It must be operational by the midpoint of the tribulation. I say this because Jesus, in His Olivet Discourse, warned that the antichrist will desecrate the temple at this time, setting up an image of himself within the structure (Matthew 24:15-16; see also Daniel 9:27; 12:11).

Even today, we hear reports that various Jewish individuals and groups have been working behind the scenes to prepare various materials for the future temple, including priestly robes, temple tapestries, and worship utensils. The Jewish Sanhedrin is currently raising money and drawing up architectural plans for the rebuilding of the temple. The fulfillment of this temple prophecy seems to be on the not-too-distant horizon.

The "Signs of the Times" Will Affirm that the End Times Have Arrived

A *sign of the times* is an event of prophetic significance that points to the end times. Jesus warned that certain signs would transpire as the tribulation period starts to unfold (Matthew 24). These include a significant increase in earthquakes, famine, pestilence, and signs in the heavens. There will also be a great escalation in false Christs, false prophets, false teachers, and false apostles—along with a considerable parallel increase in apostasy. The arrival of such signs will be clear proof that the end times have arrived.

The increase in false Christs and false prophets will prepare the way for the emergence of the ultimate false Christ (the antichrist) and the ultimate false prophet.

It is interesting to see how the signs of the times in Jesus's Olivet Discourse (Matthew 24) line up with the seal judgments in the book of Revelation (Revelation 6):

THE OLIVET DISCOURSE (MATTHEW 24)	THE SEVEN SEAL JUDGMENTS (REVELATION 6)
the rise of false Christs (verses 4-5)	*first seal:* the rise of the antichrist (verses 1-2)
wars and rumors of wars (verse 6)	*second seal:* peace is taken from the earth (verses 3-4)
famines (verse 7)	*third seal:* escalation of food costs, famine (verses 5-6)
earthquakes (verse 7)	*sixth seal:* a great earthquake (verses 12-14)

The 144,000 Jewish Evangelists Will Preach Worldwide

Revelation 7 and 14 refer to 144,000 Jewish men who come to faith in Jesus sometime after the rapture of the church. They will fulfill the mandate originally given to the Jewish nation to share the good news of God with people all around the world (see Isaiah 42:6; 43:10). God will "seal" (divinely protect) these evangelists as they carry out their service for Him during the tribulation (Revelation 14:1-4; see also 2 Corinthians 1:22; Ephesians 1:13; 4:30). They apparently begin their work early in the first half of the tribulation period.

God's Two Prophetic Witnesses Will Engage in Ministry

Aside from the 144,000 Jewish evangelists, God will also raise up two mighty prophets who will testify to the one true God with astounding power. Their miracles are reminiscent of Elijah (1 Kings 17; Malachi 4:5) and Moses (Exodus 7–11)—the two most celebrated personalities of the Old Testament.

Why two prophetic witnesses? Old Testament law stipulated that two witnesses were necessary to confirm a testimony (see Deuteronomy 17:6; 19:15; Matthew 18:16; John 8:17; Hebrews 10:28). These witnesses will engage in their ministry during the first half of the tribulation, just like the 144,000 Jewish evangelists.

The Lamb—Jesus Christ—Will Unleash the Seven Seal Judgments

The seven-sealed scroll is a scroll of judgments. As each new seal is opened, a new judgment is unleashed on the earth during the first half of the tribulation period. The only person worthy in heaven to take this scroll and open its seals is Jesus Christ (Revelation 5). This means that the judgments that fall upon the world during these years have their ultimate source in Jesus Christ.

The seal judgments include the rise of the antichrist, the outbreak of war, widespread famine, massive casualties, a devastating earthquake, and even worse judgments (Revelation 6). Things will progressively go from bad to worse.

Martyrdom Will Escalate Dramatically

The rapture of Christians will already have taken place before the tribulation period (1 Thessalonians 1:10; 4:13-17; 5:9; Revelation 3:10). That said, multitudes of other people will become believers during the seven-year tribulation (Matthew 25:31-46; Revelation 7:9-10). The forces of the antichrist will martyr many of these converts (Revelation 6:9-11). Christ urges these new believers to stand firm in their faith and not fear martyrdom (Revelation 2:10). Death is not to be feared. *They will live forever by His side.*

Christ Will Unleash the Seven Trumpet Judgments

Things will continue to go from bad to worse during the tribulation period. The seventh seal judgment, initiated by Christ, will bring about seven new trumpet judgments. These trumpet judgments include hail and fire falling on the earth, a fiery mountain plummeting into the sea, a star (asteroid) falling from heaven and making a deep impact on the earth, various cosmic disturbances, hideous demons torturing humans, fallen angels killing a third of humankind, and even worse judgments. This will be a time of horrific suffering on the earth.

A False Religion Emanating from New Babylon Will Dominate the World

A powerful false religion associated with New Babylon will arise early in the tribulation period that will exercise global influence (Revelation 17:15). It will be utterly unfaithful to the truth and will therefore be called a spiritual "prostitute" (verses 1,5,15-16).

This false religion will exercise substantial political clout among the nations of the world (Revelation 17:12-13). The religion will seem outwardly glorious while being inwardly corrupt (verse 4). It will persecute those who follow Christ during the first half of the tribulation period (verse 6). It will spew out an endless flow of deception and apostasy.

PROPHETIC EVENTS AT THE MIDPOINT OF THE TRIBULATION PERIOD

Satan Will Be Cast Out of Heaven

At the midpoint of the tribulation period, there will be a massive battle in heaven between Satan with his fallen angels and the archangel Michael with the holy angels. This angelic battle will end in Satan's ousting from heaven, being cast down to the earth, after which he will indwell—or, at the very least, fully energize—the antichrist (Revelation 12:12-13; 2 Thessalonians 2:9). Satan will be furious because he now knows his time is short. Only the last three-and-a-half years of the tribulation period remain. Satan's fury will energize and motivate the antichrist's fury, and things will continue to worsen on the earth.

The Antichrist Will Be Wounded and Seem to Resurrect

Some Bible expositors interpret Revelation 13:1-3 as saying that the antichrist will suffer a mortal head wound, die, and then literally rise from the dead. Others think he will suffer a severe wound that only *appears* to be lethal, and will then *feign* a resurrection from the dead.

Either way, people around the world will *believe* he has been resurrected from the dead. They will consequently worship him. This is no doubt part of Satan's master plan to elevate the antichrist to godhood on earth.

God's Two Prophetic Witnesses Will Be Executed by the Antichrist and Then Resurrect

The miracles performed by God's two prophetic witnesses are similar to those of Elijah (1 Kings 17; Malachi 4:5) and Moses (Exodus 7–11). They will minister during the first half of the tribulation period. Many will believe in Jesus as a result of their ministry.

Once the ministry of the two prophets is complete, the antichrist will execute them. As their bodies lay in the streets of Jerusalem, the unbelievers of the world will celebrate their deaths, giving presents to each other. Three-and-a-half days later, however, the two witnesses will be raised from the dead and ascend into heaven, and the people's celebration will turn to dread (Revelation 11:7-12).

The False Religion Associated with New Babylon Will Be Destroyed

The antichrist—along with ten kings under his authority—will now destroy the false religious system associated with New Babylon. Following this, the antichrist will come into global dominion both politically *and* religiously, demanding worship as god (Daniel 11:36-38; 2 Thessalonians 2:4; Revelation 13:8,15). The final world religion will involve worship of the antichrist alone. *No competing religious systems will be allowed.*

Meanwhile—the Antichrist Will Break His Covenant with Israel

The covenant the antichrist signed with Israel was intended to remain in effect for a full seven years. At the three-and-a-half-year mark, however, the antichrist will renege on the covenant and shut down Israel's temple sacrifices. From that point onward, the antichrist will insist that the world worship him alone (Daniel 9:27; Revelation 13:8,15-18). *No competing religious systems will be allowed.*

The Antichrist Will Desecrate the Jewish Temple

The antichrist will then desecrate the Jewish temple. He will set up an image of himself within it. Jesus referred to this as the "abomination of desolation" (Matthew 24:15 NASB). He will literally desecrate the temple with this image.

This constitutes a significant turning point. The antichrist will start out as Israel's *protector* (with a signed covenant). He will end up becoming Israel's *persecutor*. He will turn from being Israel's *defender* to being its *defiler*.

A Jewish Remnant Will Consequently Flee from Israel

Jesus warns the Jews in Jerusalem that when these horrific circumstances unfold with the antichrist—especially when he deifies himself in God's temple—they should forget about gathering their personal belongings and get out of Jerusalem immediately. They are to run for their lives. Time spent gathering things might mean the difference between life and death. Jesus warns that distress is about to escalate dramatically and rapidly for the Jewish people (Matthew 24:16-22; see also Revelation 12:5-6). Jeremiah 30:7 describes this period as "a time of trouble for my people Israel."

God Will Keep a Remnant of the Jews Safe in the Wilderness

Many of the Jews who escape Jerusalem will flee to the deserts and mountains (Matthew 24:16), perhaps in the area of Bozrah/Petra, about eighty miles south of Jerusalem. God promises to protect this remnant for the last three-and-a-half years of the tribulation period (Revelation 12:6-14).

The False Prophet Will Carry Out His Diabolical Ministry

During this time Satan will empower the false prophet to engage in what we might call Grade-B miracles—lesser than God's miracles but still impressive (see Exodus 7:11; 2 Timothy 3:8). The false prophet will engage in these miracles to induce people around the world to worship Satan's substitute for Christ—the antichrist (see Daniel 9:27; 11:31; 12:11; Matthew 24:15). These will be deceptive times.

The Antichrist Will Make War on the Saints

At this time the antichrist will engage in great persecution against not only the Jews but also followers of Jesus. He will "wage war against God's holy people" and "conquer them" (Revelation 13:7; see also Daniel 7:21). God's people will have a tough time, especially as they enter the second half of the tribulation period.

PROPHETIC EVENTS IN THE SECOND HALF OF THE TRIBULATION PERIOD

The Great Tribulation Begins

The second half of the tribulation period will be worse than the first half. Because of this, the last three-and-a-half years is called the "great tribulation" (Matthew 24:15-21; see also Daniel 9:27; Revelation 13:5). During this time, the antichrist will act as god on earth, enforcing both political and religious dominion and supremacy. This will be the worst time in all human history.

New Babylon Will Emerge as the Political and Commercial Center of the World

During the second half of the tribulation period, New Babylon will become the political and economic center of the world. Because political leaders around the world will openly embrace New Babylon, the reach of New Babylon will truly be global. Both world leaders and businesspeople will become very wealthy because of their association with New Babylon (Revelation 18:1-19).

The Antichrist and False Prophet Will Enforce the Mark of the Beast

The antichrist and the false prophet will subjugate the entire world so that those who refuse the mark of the beast cannot buy or sell (Revelation 13:16-18). This mark will be a passport to commerce.

Those who accept the mark of the beast will eat well. Those who refuse the mark of the beast—such as new believers in Jesus—will find it hard, if not impossible, to acquire food. Many of these believers will die during this time.

Because New Babylon will be the commerce center of the world during the second half of the tribulation period, it is logical to infer that a pivotal component to the success of New Babylon is the antichrist's mark of the beast. After all, the only people who will be able to sell their products to super-rich New Babylon will be those who have received the mark (Revelation 18:11-15).

Great Deception Will Continue to Escalate

Jesus warned that during the tribulation period there would be increasing deception (Matthew 24:11). The apostle Paul speaks of end-times "evil deception" rooted in "lies" (2 Thessalonians 2:9-11). Revelation 12:9 tells us that Satan—"the one deceiving the whole world"—will be highly active during this period. The antichrist's first lieutenant, the false prophet, will deceive "all the people who belong to this world" (Revelation 13:14). Truth will be a rare commodity during those days.

God Will Unleash the Bowl Judgments

The world will have already suffered the unleashing of the seal judgments and the trumpet judgments. God will now unleash the bowl judgments—the worst judgments of all (Revelation 16:1-21). People will suffer harmful and painful sores, the sea will become like blood, the rivers and springs of water will also become like blood, the sun will scorch people with fire, the world will plunge into utter darkness, the Euphrates River will dry up (preparing the way for the outbreak of Armageddon), and more. Woe to those who are upon the earth at this time.

In the next chapter, we will continue our investigation of the WHAT and WHEN of prophetic events related to the end of the tribulation period and shortly thereafter.

The Big Ideas

- The antichrist's covenant with Israel will start the tribulation period.

- Many signs of the times will confirm that the end times have arrived.

- In the first half of the tribulation, the antichrist will become a powerful political leader.

- Christ's progressively worsening judgments will fall upon the world during this time.

- Deception will run rampant.

- God's light will continue to shine in the world through the 144,000 Jewish evangelists and God's two prophetic witnesses.

- At the midpoint of the tribulation, the antichrist will exalt himself as god. After an apparent resurrection from the dead, the world will worship him. The false prophet will assist him.

- Following the antichrist's desecration of the Jewish temple, a Jewish remnant will escape Jerusalem to find refuge in the wilderness, where God will protect them.

- The second half of the tribulation period will be the "great tribulation."

- New Babylon will become the political and commercial center of the world.

- Through the mark of the beast, the antichrist will control the world economically.

- God will unleash the bowl judgments.

Questions for Reflection

1. Do the 144,000 Jewish evangelists who fearlessly proclaim the gospel of the kingdom motivate you to be a better witness for Christ in your circle of influence? How so?

2. The persecution of God's people will be widespread during the tribulation period. Can you think of a time when someone persecuted you or mocked you or spoke condescendingly of you for being a Christian? How did you respond?

12

Events at the End of (and Right After) the Tribulation

I n chapter 11 we explored the first and second halves of the tribulation period. We continue in this chapter with a focus on prophetic events that will transpire at the end of (and right after) the tribulation period.

EVENTS AT THE END OF THE TRIBULATION PERIOD

The Campaign of Armageddon Will Explode

Armageddon—a catastrophic war campaign—will explode on the scene at the end of the tribulation period (Revelation 16:14-16; see also Daniel 11:40-45; Joel 3:9-17; Zechariah 14:1-3). Countless millions of people will perish in the worst escalation of conflict ever to hit planet Earth. There are eight stages of this ongoing war campaign.

Stage One of Armageddon: The Antichrist's Allies Will Assemble for War

The antichrist's allies from around the world will gather for one purpose—*to engage in the final destruction of the Jews* (Revelation 16:12-16). Demonic spirits will inspire this attack. Satan will continue to energize the antichrist in this hatred of the Jews.

Keep in mind that Satan knows Jesus was born from Jewish lineage, and he knows that God still has a purpose and a plan for Israel. Satan's hatred of Israel is an outgrowth of his greater hatred for Christ.

Stage Two of Armageddon: Commercial and Political Babylon Will Be Destroyed

New Babylon will become a global commercial and political center in the second half of the tribulation period. The antichrist will carry out his global reign there during this time. The destruction of New Babylon—an expression God's fierce wrath (Jeremiah 50:13-14)—will leave behind nothing but a desert wasteland. New Babylon will be "devastated like Sodom and Gomorrah" (Isaiah 13:19; Jeremiah 50:40). The destruction will be all-encompassing and permanent.

Stage Three of Armageddon: Jerusalem Will Fall

Though the antichrist will know his headquarters in New Babylon has just suffered obliteration, that will not dissuade him from his Satan-inspired goal of destroying the Jewish people once and for all. He will instruct his military forces to attack Jerusalem. Zechariah 14:1-2 reveals that "all the nations" will gather to "fight against Jerusalem." I hate to say it, but since "all the nations" will participate, this must mean the United States will be a part of the invading force. Jerusalem will fall in the face of this overwhelming attack.

Stage Four of Armageddon: The Antichrist Will Move South Against the Jewish Remnant

After Jerusalem's destruction, the antichrist and his forces will move south against the Jewish remnant (Matthew 24:16; Revelation 6:12,14). We recall that this remnant escaped from Jerusalem at the midpoint of the tribulation period after the antichrist set up an image of himself inside the Jewish temple (Daniel 9:27; 11:31; Matthew 24:15-21).

These Jews took refuge in the deserts and mountains (Matthew 24:16)—perhaps in Bozrah or Petra, about eighty miles south of Jerusalem. From an earthly perspective, this remnant of Jews will be utterly defenseless against the overwhelming forces of the antichrist.

Stage Five of Armageddon: The Endangered Jewish Remnant Will Turn to Jesus

Things will seem hopeless for the Jewish remnant in the face of the overwhelming forces of the antichrist. But now something amazing will take place. God will remove the spiritual blindness of the Jews (see Romans 9–11). Their spiritual eyes will now be able to perceive the truth. The Jews will finally recognize Jesus as their beloved Messiah. The remnant will experience regeneration by turning to their Messiah, Jesus Christ (Hosea 6:1-3; see also Joel 2:28-29; Zechariah 12:2–13:1). And once regenerated, they will cry out to Jesus for deliverance in the face of imminent annihilation from the forces of the antichrist.

Heads up! This does not mean that every Jew on planet Earth has now trusted in Jesus. The remnant in the wilderness that trusts in Christ has now become saved, but there will also no doubt be other Jews scattered around the world who have not trusted in Christ for salvation.

Stage Six of Armageddon: Jesus Will Return in Glory

Jesus will promptly answer the prayers of the Jewish remnant. The divine Messiah will return personally to rescue the remnant from destruction. Every eye will see Him (Revelation 1:7). Christ will come as the King of kings and Lord of lords. None will be able to withstand Him (Revelation 19:11-16). The forces of the antichrist will be as nothing in the face His Royal Majesty.

CHRIST'S SECOND COMING	
Christ will come visibly.	Acts 1:9-11
Christ will come from heaven.	1 Thessalonians 1:10
Every eye will see Him.	Zechariah 12:10; Revelation 1:7
Christ will come back on the clouds of heaven.	Matthew 26:64
Christ will come in great glory.	Matthew 16:27; 25:31; Mark 8:38; Luke 9:26

Stage Seven of Armageddon: The Final Battle Will Erupt

Jesus will confront the antichrist and his military forces and will effortlessly slay them: "The Lord Jesus will slay him with the breath of his mouth and destroy him by the splendor of his coming" (2 Thessalonians 2:8).

Jesus will essentially say "drop dead," and the forces of the antichrist will experience instant death. Their attack against His chosen people will yield a complete forfeiture of their lives. They will be no match for the King of kings and Lord of lords (Revelation 19:16). The Jewish Messiah will obliterate all opposition.

Stage Eight of Armageddon: Christ Will Victoriously Ascend the Mount of Olives

Scripture reveals: "On that day his feet will stand on the Mount of Olives, east of Jerusalem. And the Mount of Olives will split apart, making a wide valley running from east to west. Half the mountain will move toward the north and half toward the south" (Zechariah 14:4). I find it fascinating that topographical upheavals often accompany God's great acts of judgment in the Bible (see Micah 1:2-4; Nahum 1:5; Revelation 16:18-21).

EVENTS RIGHT AFTER THE TRIBULATION PERIOD

There Will Be a 75-Day Interim Between the End of the Tribulation Period and the Beginning of the Millennial Kingdom

Scripture reveals there will be a 75-day interim between the end of the tribulation period and the beginning of the millennial kingdom. Here's how we arrive at the number: Daniel 12:12 states: "Blessed is he who waits and arrives at the 1,335 days." We already know that the second half of the tribulation period is 1260 days (or three-and-a-half years). So, here's some simple math: 1335 minus 1260 equals 75.

Since the millennial kingdom has not yet begun, this can only mean there is a 75-day time span between the end of the tribulation period and the beginning of the millennial kingdom. A number of events apparently take place during this interim period.

The Judgment of the Nations Will Take Place During the 75-Day Interim

Matthew 25:31-46 describes the judgment of the nations, which will immediately follow the second coming of Christ after the tribulation period. Believers and unbelievers from among the nations are pictured as sheep and goats. According to Matthew 25:32, they are intermingled and require separation by a special judgment. The sheep (believers) will enter Christ's thousand-year millennial kingdom. The goats will depart into eternal fire.

Christ will judge the Gentiles according to how they treated His "brothers" during the tribulation period. In Christ's reckoning, treating His brothers kindly is the same as treating Him kindly. Treating His brothers with contempt is the same as treating Him with contempt.

Jesus will thus commend the righteous this way: "I was hungry and you gave me food, I was thirsty and you gave me drink, I was a stranger and you welcomed me, I was naked and you clothed me, I was sick and you visited me, I was in prison and you came to me" (Matthew 25:35-36 ESV). Conversely, Jesus will condemn the unrighteous this way: "I was hungry and you gave me no food, I was thirsty and you gave me no drink, I was a stranger and you did not welcome me, naked and you did not clothe me, sick and in prison and you did not visit me" (25:42-43 ESV).

A comparison of this passage with the details of the tribulation suggests that the "brothers" are the 144,000 Jewish evangelists mentioned in Revelation 7. These are Christ's Jewish brothers who faithfully bear witness of Him during the tribulation.

Even though the antichrist and the false prophet will wield economic control over the world during the tribulation period (Revelation 13), God will still be at work. God's redeemed (the sheep) will come to the aid of Christ's Jewish brethren with food and water (and meet other needs) as these Jews bear witness to Christ all around the world. The sheep will be invited to enter Christ's millennial kingdom.

These saved Gentiles will not yet receive their resurrection bodies. They will enter the kingdom in their mortal bodies and continue to get married and have babies throughout the millennium. Though longevity will characterize the millennial kingdom, both mortal Jews and Gentiles will continue to age and die (Isaiah 65:20). They will be resurrected following the millennial kingdom (Revelation 20:4).

The Judgment of the Jews Will Take Place During the 75-Day Interim

Christ will not only judge the Gentiles during the 75-day interim, He will also judge the Jews during this time (Ezekiel 20:34-38). This judgment will take place after the Lord has gathered the Jews from all around the earth to Israel. He will purge out all the rebels—those who have refused to turn to Him for salvation.

Believers among the gathered Jews will be invited to enter Christ's millennial kingdom. There they will enjoy the blessings of the new covenant, the Davidic covenant, and the Abrahamic covenant (Ezekiel 20:37; Jeremiah 31:31; Matthew 25:1-30).

These saved Jews will not yet receive their resurrection bodies. They will enter the kingdom in their mortal bodies and be able to get married and have babies during the millennium just as their Gentile counterparts will (Matthew 25:46). Though they will experience long lives in the millennial kingdom, both mortal Jews and Gentiles will continue to age and die (Isaiah 65:20). After the millennium, they will be resurrected (Revelation 20:4).

The Divine Bridegroom and His Bride (the Church) Will Enjoy a Marriage Feast During the 75-Day Interim

Scripture often refers to the relationship between Christ and the church using a marriage motif, with Christ being the Bridegroom and the church the Bride (Matthew 9:15; 22:2-14; 25:1-13; Mark 2:19-20; Luke 5:34-35; 14:15-24; John 3:29). There were three phases in Hebrew weddings:

1. The bride became betrothed to the bridegroom.

2. The bridegroom came to claim his bride after preparing a place to live in his father's house.

3. The groom, bride, and family celebrated a marriage supper—a feast lasting several days, even up to a week.

We see these phases in Christ's relationship to the church or Bride of Christ:

1. As individuals living during the church age come to salvation, they become a part of the church, the Bride of Christ, betrothed to the divine Bridegroom.

2. The Bridegroom (Jesus Christ) will come to claim His Bride at the rapture, at which time He will take the Bride to heaven, the Father's house, where He has prepared a place to live (John 14:1-3). The actual marriage will take place in heaven following the rapture.

3. The marriage feast of the Lamb will take place on earth during the 75-day interval between the end of the tribulation period and the beginning of the millennial kingdom. It will be an awesome spectacle.

THE BRIDEGROOM AND BRIDE OF CHRIST	
The church is a virgin bride awaiting her heavenly Bridegroom.	2 Corinthians 11:2; Revelation 19:7-9
Jesus—the Bridegroom—is preparing a home for the Bride in His Father's house (heaven).	John 14:1-3
The marriage of the Lamb takes place.	Revelation 19:7-16
The marriage feast of the Lamb takes place.	Revelation 19:9

Finally, Preparations for the Millennial Kingdom Will Take Place During the 75-day Interim

Before the millennial kingdom begins, preparations will first be made. These will take place during the 75-day interim:

1. The antichrist and the false prophet will no longer be permitted to attack God's people. They will be cast alive into the lake of fire (Revelation 19:20).

2. Satan will be bound in the bottomless pit for a thousand years (Revelation 20:2).

3. Christ will then set up the governmental structure of the coming millennial kingdom (2 Timothy 2:12; Revelation 20:4-6). Faithful Christians will reign with Christ, and Christ will no doubt hand out governmental assignments at this time.

4. Tribulation saints who were martyred by the antichrist will be resurrected from the dead. They, too, will take part in reigning with Christ for a thousand years (Revelation 20:4).

REIGNING WITH CHRIST	
Believers are a kingdom of priests and will reign with Christ.	Revelation 5:10; 20:6
If we endure, we will reign with Christ.	2 Timothy 2:12
Christ's martyrs will reign with Him.	Revelation 20:4
Overcoming Christians will sit on the throne with Christ.	Revelation 3:21
Christ's servants will reign forever.	Revelation 22:5

The Big Issues

- Armageddon—a catastrophic war campaign—will explode on the scene at the end of the tribulation period.

- New Babylon will be destroyed.

- The antichrist will destroy Jerusalem. He will then move his forces toward the Jewish remnant in the wilderness.

- The Jewish remnant will recognize Jesus as their divine Messiah and ask Him for deliverance.

- Jesus will come again in glory and deliver the Jewish remnant. He will destroy the forces of the antichrist.

- During a 75-day interim between the end of the tribulation period and the beginning of the millennial kingdom, Jesus will judge the Gentile nations, judge the Jews, celebrate a marriage feast with His Bride (the previously raptured church), and make necessary preparations for the millennial kingdom.

Questions for Reflection

1. Do you think you live more like a citizen of earth or a citizen of heaven? How so?

2. Is your lifestyle befitting a bride awaiting the soon appearance of her Bridegroom? Why or why not?

3. Has your study of biblical prophecy bolstered your faith in God and your confidence in the Bible? If so, how?

13

Events in the Millennial Kingdom

In chapter 12 we explored events that will take place at the end of—and right after—the tribulation period. We continue in the present chapter with a focus on prophetic events that will transpire during Christ's millennial kingdom.

Christ's Millennial Kingdom Will Begin

Following Christ's second coming, and after the 75-day interim period has passed, He will set up His thousand-year kingdom on earth. Theologians call this the millennial kingdom. (The Latin term *mille* means "a thousand." *Millennial kingdom* thus refers to a thousand-year kingdom.) There are many prophecies of this kingdom scattered throughout Scripture (Revelation 20:2-7; Psalm 2:6-9; Isaiah 65:18-23; Jeremiah 31:12-14,31-37; Ezekiel 34:25-29; 37:1-13; 40–48; Daniel 2:35; 7:13-14; Joel 2:21-27; Amos 9:13-14; Micah 4:1-7; Zephaniah 3:9-20).

Those Who Became Believers During the Tribulation Will Enter the Millennial Kingdom

Believing Gentiles will enter the millennial kingdom in their mortal bodies (Matthew 25:34,46). Likewise, the redeemed remnant among the Jews will enter the millennial kingdom in their mortal bodies (Ezekiel 20:34-38).

Longevity will characterize the millennial kingdom. But Scripture reveals that both mortal Jews and Gentiles will continue to grow old and die (Isaiah 65:20). Scripture also reveals that married couples among both groups will continue to have children throughout the millennium. All who die during this time will be resurrected at the end of the millennium (Revelation 20:4).

While believers alone enter Christ's kingdom, some of the children of these believers will not become believers. After a few years have passed, there will be people—born during the early days of the millennium—who will grow to adulthood rejecting the Savior-King in their hearts (though outwardly obeying Him). They can remain in Christ's kingdom so long as they render external obedience.

God Will Spiritually Restore Israel and Will Fulfill Land Promises to Israel

The new covenant, summarized in Jeremiah 31:31-34, promises the spiritual regeneration of Israel:

> "The day is coming," says the LORD, "when I will make a new covenant with the people of Israel and Judah. This covenant will not be like the one I made with their ancestors when I took them by the hand and brought them out of the land of Egypt. They broke that covenant, though I loved them as a husband loves his wife," says the LORD.
>
> "But this is the new covenant I will make with the people of Israel after those days," says the LORD. "I will put my instructions deep within them, and I will write them on their hearts. I will be their God, and they will be my people. And they will not need to teach their neighbors, nor will they need to teach their relatives, saying, 'You should know the LORD.' For everyone, from the least to the greatest, will know me already," says the LORD. "And I will forgive their wickedness, and I will never again remember their sins."

The new covenant promises the necessary internal power for the Jewish people to obey God's commands—something that the Mosaic covenant of the law could never accomplish. This wonderful covenant promises a complete national regeneration of Israel, and every

Jew that enters the millennial kingdom will know the Lord (see Isaiah 29:22-24; 30:18-22; 44:1-5; 45:17; Jeremiah 24:7; 50:19-20; Ezekiel 11:19-20; 36:25-27; Hosea 1:10–2:1; 14:4-8; Joel 2:28-32; Micah 7:8-20; Zephaniah 3:9-13; Romans 11:25-27).

Israel will experience not only regeneration in fulfillment of the new covenant (Jeremiah 31:31-34), but also a regathering to their land. This is based on the land covenant (Deuteronomy 29:1–30:20), which is eternal and unconditional. That covenant promised that even though Israel would suffer dispersion worldwide, God would regather the Jews and restore them to the land (Isaiah 43:5-7; Jeremiah 16:14-18). This restoration to the land will ultimately take place in Christ's millennial kingdom.

We also recall the specific land promises God made to Abraham in the Abrahamic covenant: "The LORD made a covenant with Abram that day and said, 'I have given this land to your descendants, all the way from the border of Egypt to the great Euphrates River—the land now occupied by the Kenites, Kenizzites, Kadmonites, Hittites, Perizzites, Rephaites, Amorites, Canaanites, Girgashites, and Jebusites'" (Genesis 15:18-21).

The land promises God made to Abraham were later reaffirmed to Isaac (Genesis 26:3-4), to Jacob (Genesis 28:13-14), and then repeated in Psalm 105:8-11. God is a promise-keeper (Joshua 23:14; Psalm 146:6; Hebrews 10:23). Israel will come into full possession of the land, just as God promised.

Christ, the Jews, and Even Gentiles Will Build a Millennial Temple

Ezekiel 40–48 speaks of the building of a millennial temple (see also Joel 3:18; Isaiah 2:3; 60:13) and the institution of millennial animal sacrifices (see also Isaiah 56:7; 60:7; Jeremiah 33:17-18; Zechariah 14:19-21). The millennial temple will be the final temple for Israel. Its dimensions make it significantly larger than any other temple in Israel's history.

This massive temple will represent God's presence among His people during the millennium (see Ezekiel 37:26-27). The restoration of

Israel as a nation will also entail a restoration of God's presence (and glory) reentering the temple and being with His people visibly. This temple will also be a worship center of Jesus Christ during the entire millennium.

The temple will be constructed at the beginning of the messianic kingdom (Ezekiel 37:26-28) by Christ (Zechariah 6:12-13), by redeemed Jews (Ezekiel 43:10-11), and even by representatives from the Gentile nations (Zechariah 6:15; Haggai 2:7). All join together in its construction.

Many wonder why animal sacrifices will be restored in the millennial kingdom. The purpose of the sacrifices is only to remove ceremonial uncleanness and prevent defilement from polluting the purity of the temple environment. Such ceremonial cleansing will be necessary because Yahweh (God) will again be dwelling on the earth amid sinful—and therefore unclean—mortal people.

Remember, these people will survive the tribulation period and will enter the millennial kingdom *in their mortal bodies*—still in full possession of their sin natures, even though redeemed by Christ as believers. The sacrifices will thus remove any ceremonial uncleanness in the temple.

Seen in this light, the sacrifices should not be seen as a return to the Mosaic law. The law is forever antiquated in Jesus Christ (Romans 6:14-15; 7:1-6; 1 Corinthians 9:20-21; 2 Corinthians 3:7-11; Galatians 4:1-7; 5:18; Hebrews 8:13; 10:1-14). The sacrifices relate only to removing ritual impurities in the temple, as fallen-though-redeemed human beings remain on earth.

Christ Will Reign from the Davidic Throne

God made a covenant with David in which He promised that one of his descendants would rule forever on the throne of David (2 Samuel 7:12-13; 22:51). This is an example of an unconditional covenant. It did not depend on David for its fulfillment.

The Davidic covenant finds its ultimate fulfillment in Jesus Christ, who was born from the line of David (Matthew 1:1). Scripture often affirms that Christ will rule from the throne of David during the millennial kingdom (Ezekiel 36:1-12; Micah 4:1-5; Zephaniah 3:14-20; Zechariah 14:1-21). This reign will extend beyond the Jews to include the Gentile nations. Christ's government will be centered in Jerusalem (Isaiah 2:1-3; see also Jeremiah 3:17; Ezekiel 48:30-35; Joel 3:16-17; Micah 4:1,6-8; Zechariah 8:2-3). It will be perfect and effective (Isaiah 9:6-7), it will be global (Psalm 2:6-9; Daniel 7:14), and it will bring lasting global peace (Micah 4:3-4).

Resurrected Believers Will Reign with Christ

Scripture promises that Christ will gloriously reign from the Davidic throne. As noted previously, however, Scripture also promises that faithful believers will reign with Christ. In 2 Timothy 2:12, for example, the apostle Paul instructs, "If we endure hardship, we will reign with him." Those who endure through trials will one day rule with Christ in His future kingdom.

Revelation 5:10 likewise reveals that believers—God's faithful bondservants—"will reign on the earth." While this verse specifically refers to faithful believers reigning with Christ in the millennial kingdom on earth, this reign actually extends beyond the millennial kingdom into the eternal state. Revelation 22:5 affirms that faithful believers "will reign forever and ever." Luke 19 reveals that a believer's position in the heavenly government will be commensurate with his or her faithful service to God during mortal earthly life.

Reigning with Christ appears to include judging the angels in some capacity. In 1 Corinthians 6:2-3, the apostle Paul asks, "Don't you realize that someday we believers will judge the world?...Don't you realize that we will judge angels?"

Christ Will Bring Great Physical Blessings in the Millennial Kingdom

Scripture promises that Christ will bring great physical blessings to those who live during His millennial kingdom:

PHYSICAL BLESSINGS IN CHRIST'S MILLENNIAL KINGDOM	
People will live in a blessed and enhanced environment.	Isaiah 35:1-2
There will be plenty of rain and hence plenty of food for animals.	Isaiah 30:23-24
All animals will live in harmony with each other and with humans, their predatory and carnivorous natures having been removed.	Isaiah 11:6-7
Longevity among human beings will be greatly increased.	Isaiah 65:20
Physical infirmities and illnesses will be removed.	Isaiah 29:18
Prosperity will prevail, resulting in joy and gladness.	Jeremiah 31:12-14

Christ Will Bring Great Spiritual Blessings in the Millennial Kingdom

Scripture promises that Christ will bring great spiritual blessings to those who live during His millennial kingdom:

SPIRITUAL BLESSINGS IN CHRIST'S MILLENNIAL KINGDOM	
Everyone on earth will know the Lord.	Isaiah 11:9
Satan, now bound in the bottomless pit, will not be around to harass people.	Revelation 20:1-3
The Holy Spirit will be present with all believers.	Ezekiel 36:27; 37:14

SPIRITUAL BLESSINGS IN CHRIST'S MILLENNIAL KINGDOM	
The Holy Spirit will be "poured out on us from heaven."	Isaiah 32:15
Righteousness will prevail around the world.	Isaiah 46:13; 51:5; 60:21
Obedience to the Lord will prevail.	Psalm 22:27; Jeremiah 31:33
Holiness will prevail.	Isaiah 35:8-10; Joel 3:17
Faithfulness will prevail.	Psalm 85:10-11; Zechariah 8:3
The world's residents will unify in their worship of the Messiah.	Malachi 1:11; Zephaniah 3:9; Zechariah 8:23
God's presence will be made manifest.	Ezekiel 37:27-28; Zechariah 2:10-13

The Big Issues

- Christ will set up the long-anticipated millennial kingdom.

- People who become believers during the tribulation will enter the millennial kingdom in their mortal bodies.

- God will restore Israel spiritually.

- God will restore Israel to their land.

- Christ will reign for a thousand years on the Davidic throne. Faithful believers will reign with Him in varying capacities.

- Christ will bring both physical and spiritual blessings upon all who live during the millennial kingdom—both Jews and Gentiles.

Questions for Reflection

1. While Christ's reign in the millennial kingdom is yet future, does Christ presently have free reign on the throne of your heart? What changes might you want to make in your life?

2. What does it mean to you personally that God is a promise-keeper? (Try to be specific.)

14

Events Prior to and During the Eternal State

In chapter 13, we focused attention on the millennial kingdom. We continue in this chapter with a focus on prophetic events prior to and during the eternal state, which will follow the millennial kingdom.

Satan Will Lead One Final Revolt Against God and His People

Satan will be quarantined in the bottomless pit—"the Abyss"—during Christ's thousand-year millennial kingdom. In Revelation 20:1-3, we read:

> I saw an angel coming down from heaven with the key to the bottomless pit and a heavy chain in his hand. He seized the dragon—that old serpent, who is the devil, Satan—and bound him in chains for a thousand years. The angel threw him into the bottomless pit, which he then shut and locked so Satan could not deceive the nations anymore until the thousand years were finished. Afterward he must be released for a little while.

Revelation 20:7-9 then warns:

> When the thousand years come to an end, Satan will be let out of his prison. He will go out to deceive the nations...He will gather them together for battle—a mighty army, as numberless as sand along the seashore. And I saw them

as they went up on the broad plain of the earth and sur-
rounded God's people and the beloved city.

The rebels who will join Satan in this futile act of rebellion will be
unbelievers who live in the millennial kingdom. I remind you that
only redeemed Jews and redeemed Gentiles initially enter the millennial kingdom in their mortal bodies (still possessing a sinful nature).
Some of their children, grandchildren, and great-grandchildren *will
not* be believers. By the time a thousand years have passed, there will
be many unbelievers who give in to their sinful nature and join Satan
in this last rebellion.

SATAN—REBEL, DECEIVER, LIAR, MURDERER, ATTACKER	
Rebelled against God prior to the creation of humankind	Isaiah 14:12-15; Ezekiel 28:13-18
Masquerades as an angel of light	2 Corinthians 11:14
Deceives the whole world	Revelation 12:9
Is a liar and murderer	John 8:44
Gathers the armies of the world at Armageddon	Revelation 16:13-16
Gathers rebels against God after the millennial kingdom	Revelation 20:7-10

God Will Instantly Defeat the Rebellion and Cast Satan into the Lake of Fire

We read in Revelation 20:9b-10:

> Fire from heaven came down on the attacking armies and
> consumed them... Then the devil, who had deceived them,
> was thrown into the fiery lake of burning sulfur, joining the
> beast and the false prophet. There they will be tormented
> day and night forever and ever.

Fire is a common mode of God's judgment in Bible times (Genesis 19:24; Exodus 9:23-24; Leviticus 9:24; 10:2; Numbers 11:1; 16:35; 26:10; 1 Kings 18:38; 2 Kings 1:10-14; 1 Chronicles 21:26; 2 Chronicles 7:1-3; Psalm 11:6). God will squash the rebellion instantly. The attack will stand no chance of success.

The Second Resurrection Will Precede the Great White Throne Judgment

The "second resurrection" will take place in preparation for the great white throne judgment—the judgment of the wicked dead. We recall that during His earthly ministry, Jesus soberly announced: "The time is coming when all the dead in their graves will hear the voice of God's Son, and they will rise again. Those who have done good will rise to experience eternal life, and those who have continued in evil will rise to experience judgment" (John 5:28-29).

In keeping with this, Revelation makes reference to the first resurrection and the second resurrection (see Revelation 20:5-6,11-15). These are *types* of resurrections. The first resurrection is the resurrection of Christians. God's people are resurrected at different times—some at the rapture, some after the tribulation period, and some at the end of the millennial kingdom. All of these are part of the first resurrection. The second resurrection is the resurrection of the wicked, in preparation for their judgment before Christ (Revelation 20:13). The unsaved dead of all time—regardless of what century they lived in—will be resurrected to face Christ.

The Wicked Dead Will Face Christ at the Great White Throne Judgment

Revelation 20:12 tells us: "I saw the dead, both great and small, standing before God's throne. And the books were opened, including the Book of Life. And the dead were judged according to what they had done, as recorded in the books." These books detail the lives of the unsaved and will supply the evidence to substantiate the divine verdict of a destiny in the lake of fire. Christ will examine the unbelievers' actions (Matthew 16:27), their words (Matthew 12:37), and even their thoughts and motives (Luke 8:17; Romans 2:16). It will be a horrific scene.

GOD'S JUDGMENT	
After death comes judgment	Hebrews 9:27
Based on truth	Psalm 96:13; Romans 2:1-2
Believers judged by Christ	1 Corinthians 3:10-15; 2 Corinthians 5:10
Day of judgment coming	2 Peter 3:7
Every deed judged	Ecclesiastes 12:14
Great white throne judgment	Revelation 20:12
Inevitable	Jeremiah 44:15-28
Judgment awaits all	Matthew 12:36; Romans 14:10,12
Motivates holiness	2 Corinthians 5:9-10; 2 Peter 3:11,14
Motivates repentance	Acts 17:30-31
Nations judged at second coming	Joel 3:2; Matthew 25:31-46
Nothing kept secret from God	Hebrews 4:13

The Lake of Fire Will Be Populated by the Wicked

Following the great white throne judgment, the wicked dead will be cast into the lake of fire. Scripture characterizes their existence in the lake of fire as involving weeping and gnashing of teeth (Matthew 13:41-42), condemnation (Matthew 12:36-37), destruction (Philippians 1:28), eternal punishment (Matthew 25:46), separation from God's presence (2 Thessalonians 1:8-9), and tribulation and distress (Romans 2:9).

Scripture also reveals there will be degrees of punishment in the lake of fire. These degrees of punishment will be commensurate with the degrees of sinfulness (see Matthew 10:15; 11:20-24; 16:27; Luke

12:47-48; 20:47; John 19:11; Revelation 20:12-13; 22:12). All lake-of-fire residents will suffer torment day and night forever.

DEGREES OF PUNISHMENT IN THE LAKE OF FIRE	
Each judged on what one has done	Revelation 20:12-13
God will recompense everyone	Revelation 22:12
More bearable for some than others	Matthew 10:15
Repay each person	Matthew 16:27
Some are punished only lightly	Luke 12:48
Some are more severely punished	Luke 12:47

The Old Heavens and the Old Earth Will Be Destroyed

God placed a curse on the earth following Adam and Eve's sin against God (Genesis 3:17-18). Romans 8:20 affirms that "all creation was subjected to God's curse." Redeemed humans obviously cannot live eternally in a cursed creation. Hence, the earth—along with the first and second heavens (the earth's atmosphere and the stellar universe)—will be dissolved by fire. The old order will be dissolved to make way for the new heavens and earth (Psalm 102:25-26; Isaiah 51:6; Matthew 24:35).

We do well to remember that Satan has long carried out his evil schemes on earth (Ephesians 2:2). The stains resulting from his extended presence must therefore be purged. Satan will have no place in the new heavens and the new earth. God will remove all evidence of his influence when He dissolves the earth and the heavens (2 Peter 3:7-13).

God Will Create a New Heavens and a New Earth

Although the present universe—stained by sin—will be destroyed, God will create new heavens and a new earth for us to dwell in forever.

All vestiges of the curse and Satan's presence will be utterly and permanently removed from all creation. All things will be made new, and how blessed it will be!

The Greek word used to designate the newness of the cosmos is *kainos*. This word means "new in nature" or "new in quality." Hence the phrase "new heavens and a new earth" refers not to a cosmos that is totally other than the present cosmos. Rather, the new cosmos will stand in continuity with the present cosmos, but it will be completely renewed and renovated (Revelation 21:1,5). In keeping with this, Matthew 19:28 speaks of a new world. Acts 3:21 speaks of a coming restoration.

All this means that resurrected believers will live on a resurrected earth in a resurrected universe! The new heavens and earth, like our newness in Christ, will be regenerated, glorified, free from the curse of sin, and eternal. The new earth—a renewed and eternal earth—will be adapted to the vast moral and physical changes that the eternal state requires. Everything is new in the eternal state. Everything is according to God's glorious nature. The new heavens and the new earth are brought into blessed conformity with all that God is—in a state of fixed bliss and absolute perfection.

The New Jerusalem Will Rest Upon the New Earth

The New Jerusalem—a heavenly city—will be our eternal residence. The description of the New Jerusalem in Revelation is astounding. We witness such transcendent splendor that the human mind can scarcely take it in. This is a scene of ecstatic joy and fellowship of sinless angels and redeemed, glorified human beings. The voice of the one identified as the Alpha and the Omega, the beginning and the end, utters a climactic declaration: "Look, I am making everything new!" (Revelation 21:5). The words of Revelation 21 and 22 represent a human attempt to describe the indescribable.

In Revelation 21:11-21 we read of the New Jerusalem:

> It shone with the glory of God and sparkled like a precious stone—like jasper as clear as crystal. The city wall was

broad and high, with twelve gates guarded by twelve angels. And the names of the twelve tribes of Israel were written on the gates. There were three gates on each side—east, north, south, and west. The wall of the city had twelve foundation stones, and on them were written the names of the twelve apostles of the Lamb...

The wall was made of jasper, and the city was pure gold, as clear as glass. The wall of the city was built on foundation stones inlaid with twelve precious stones: the first was jasper, the second sapphire, the third agate, the fourth emerald, the fifth onyx, the sixth carnelian, the seventh chrysolite, the eighth beryl, the ninth topaz, the tenth chrysoprase, the eleventh jacinth, the twelfth amethyst.

The twelve gates were made of pearls—each gate from a single pearl! And the main street was pure gold, as clear as glass.

The New Jerusalem reflects the incredible glory of God. The mention of transparent gold reveals that the city will transmit the glory of God in the form of light without hindrance. The human imagination is incapable of fathoming the immeasurably resplendent glory of God that will be perpetually on display in the eternal city. This is especially so when we consider that the eternal city will overflow with many precious stones.

This will be a literal city, a real place where real resurrected people and a holy God will dwell together. A city has dwellings, order (government), bustling activity, various kinds of gatherings, and much more. There is no warrant for taking the descriptions of the New Jerusalem in Scripture as merely symbolic. Every description we have of the New Jerusalem in the Bible implies a real place of residence—albeit a resplendently glorious residence.

THE NEW JERUSALEM	
Christ is building it for us.	John 14:1-3
It is always lighted.	Revelation 22:5
It measures nearly two million square miles.	Revelation 21:16
The river of the water of life flows down its main street.	Revelation 22:1-2
It has twelve foundations with the names of the twelve apostles.	Revelation 21:14
It has twelve gates, with twelve angels at the gates.	Revelation 21:12

We Will Be Privileged to Enjoy a Grand Reversal

God will bring about an incredible grand reversal for us:

- In the beginning, God created the heavens and the earth (Genesis 1:1). In the eternal state, a new heavens and a new earth await us (Revelation 21:1-2).

- In the beginning, the sun and moon were created as "two great lights" (Genesis 1:16-17). The eternal state entails an eternal city where there is no longer any need for such light, for the glory of God lights up the eternal city of the redeemed (Revelation 21:23; 22:5).

- In the beginning, God created the night (Genesis 1:5). The eternal state involves a nightless eternity (Revelation 22:5).

- In the beginning, God created the seas (Genesis 1:10). The new earth in the eternal state will no longer have a sea (Revelation 21:1).

- In the beginning, human beings succumbed to Satan's temptations (Genesis 3:1-4). In the eternal state, Satan will be eternally quarantined from the people of God (Revelation 20:10).

- In the beginning, God pronounced a curse following humankind's fall into sin (Genesis 3:17). In the eternal state, there will be no more curse (Revelation 22:3).

- In the beginning, paradise was lost (Genesis 3:23-24). In the eternal state, paradise will be gloriously restored for redeemed humans (Revelation 2:7).

- In the beginning, Adam and Eve were barred from the tree of life (Genesis 3:22-24). In the eternal state, redeemed humans will enjoy restoration to the tree of life (Revelation 2:7; 22:2,14,19).

- In the beginning, tears, death, and mourning entered human existence (Genesis 2:17; 29:11; 37:34). In the eternal state, tears, death, and mourning will be forever absent from the redeemed (Revelation 21:4).

- In the beginning, a Redeemer was promised (Genesis 3:15). In the eternal state, the victorious Redeemer reigns (Revelation 20:1-6; 21:22-27; 22:3-5).

How wondrous it will all be!

The Big Issues

- After the millennial kingdom, Satan will lead one final revolt against God.

- God will instantly defeat the revolt and cast Satan into the lake of fire.

- God will resurrect the wicked dead, judge them, and cast them into the lake of fire.

- God will dissolve the old heavens and the old earth by fire and create a new heavens and new earth.

- An eternal city called the New Jerusalem will then rest upon the new earth. God and humankind will dwell there for all eternity.

- We will all experience a grand reversal. Everything bad will be replaced with all that is good.

Questions for Reflection

1. Think about being reunited with your Christian loved ones who are now in heaven. How does this energize you spiritually?

2. Do you make a habit of keeping a top-down perspective—a heavenly perspective? Are you presently facing any difficulties where an eternal perspective might boost your emotions?

3. What do you think about the upcoming grand reversal?

PART 4

WHERE IN THE WORLD WILL END-TIME PROPHECIES UNFOLD?

15

WHERE in the World: Part 1

We have covered a lot of ground in this book. So far, we've examined the WHO, WHAT, and WHEN of Bible prophecy. In the present chapter, we'll shift our attention to the WHERE of Bible prophecy.

Of course, I've already touched on where certain prophetic events will unfold in the world—but only in a minimalistic and somewhat disjointed way. We'll examine the details in this and the next chapter. My purpose will be to paint prophetic geography using broad strokes to give you the big picture of end-times geography.

I must remind you yet again that each category of this book—including WHERE—represents a different vantage point in our study of prophecy. Taken together, these vantage points provide a full, composite understanding of Bible prophecy.

I grant that there is some repetition along the way. But (*surprise!*) this is by design. Did you know the ancient Jews used repetition as a primary teaching tool? They used this tool because it works. The more often you are exposed to a truth—especially from different vantage points—the better you will be able to retain that truth in your mind.

One modern teaching expert tells us that "repetition is the mother of all learning." Another says that "repetition is the first principle of all learning." Yet another says that repetition is "the key to mastery." Please believe me when I tell you that repetition is your friend.

At the outset of this book, I promised you that you'd become conversant in Bible prophecy. Repetition that involves different vantage points makes this goal attainable.

Let's begin our geographical exploration with Israel and Jerusalem.

The Centrality of Israel

Israel is a mere eight thousand square miles. It is minuscule compared to the over five million square miles of Arab real estate that surrounds her.

Today Muslim extremists say their goal is to destroy the "great Satan" and the "lesser Satan" (meaning the United States and Israel). They boast that soon we will have a United States-free and Israel-free world. Some Muslim extremists have said quite pointedly that they want to "wipe Israel off the map." With Israel being so geographically small, and Muslim territories being so geographically large, one can easily understand the existential threat that exists today against Israel.

A number of Islamic organizations pose a threat against Israel. Hezbollah, for example, is a Lebanese umbrella organization of radical Islamic Shiites who hate Israel. They advocate the establishment of Shiite Islamic rule in Lebanon and the liberation of all "occupied Arab lands," including Jerusalem. Hezbollah has been relentless in vowing to destroy Israel. Iran has continuously provided financial backing to Hezbollah amounting to hundreds of millions of dollars.

Another example is Hamas, an organization that says that negotiations with the Israelis are a waste of time because the Arabs and Israelis cannot coexist. The military wing of the organization has committed countless terrorist attacks and atrocities against Israel, including hundreds of suicide bombings. Hamas has received funding from Iran, Saudi Arabia, the Gulf States, the United Arab Emirates, Syria, and Iraq.

Iran's supreme leader Ayatollah Khamenei claims that Iran has the major role to play in the destruction of Israel, and for that reason must obtain the strongest weapons possible. Khamenei has promised that Israel will not survive the next twenty-five years. With that threat in mind, it is sobering to realize that Iran is seeking to develop nuclear weapons and obtain missiles capable of delivering nuclear payloads.

Such circumstances are not a surprise to those familiar with biblical prophecy. Scripture tells us that Israel will increasingly be a sore spot in the world in the end times. In Zechariah 12:2, God prophetically affirms: "I will make Jerusalem like an intoxicating drink that makes the nearby nations stagger when they send their armies to besiege Jerusalem and Judah." The ESV translates it, "Behold, I am about to make Jerusalem a cup of staggering to all the surrounding peoples." The NIV puts it: "I am going to make Jerusalem a cup that sends all the surrounding peoples reeling." If there's one thing this verse tells us, it's that even though Israel is small, the end-times turmoil generated by this nation will affect many larger nations. The nations that surround Israel are Islamic. They are brutally anti-Semitic. We may expect plenty of "reeling" in the years to come.

Things become even more sobering when we consider the next verse—Zechariah 12:3—where God unequivocally states: "On that day I will make Jerusalem an immovable rock. All the nations will gather against it to try to move it, but *they will only hurt themselves*" (emphasis added). This means that in the end times, Jerusalem will be at the center of international controversy. Various nations will become intoxicated with a desire to possess and control Jerusalem. The nations of the world—perhaps the United Nations—will seek to internationalize Jerusalem and control its future. But Zechariah prophetically warns that all who attempt to control Jerusalem for their own purposes will quickly suffer calamity. This fact relates directly to the coming "Ezekiel Invasion" in which Russia and a coalition of Muslim nations will invade Israel and consequently be destroyed by God. Despite any temporary peace accords made with Israel, you can bank on the fact that this invasion—and the destruction of the invaders—will one day occur.

One thing is certain. Israel has a special place in God's sovereign plan of the ages. As my friend David Reagan put it:

> The Scriptures reveal the Jews as "the apple of God's eye" (Zechariah 2:8). Their land is described as "holy" (Zechariah 2:12). Their city of Jerusalem is termed the "center of the nations" (Ezekiel 5:5). They are pictured as the wayward wife of God (see Ezekiel 16 and the book of Hosea). And the Bible makes it clear that they will be the object of

both God's wrath (Jeremiah 30:7) and His grace (Zechariah 13:1) in the end times.[15]

One of the most magnificent manifestations of God's grace is His miraculous preservation of Israel for the past 2700 years. Just think about it:

- After Jerusalem and the temple were destroyed in AD 70, the Jews were dispersed to more than 130 nations around the world.

- The Jews were mistreated and relentlessly persecuted wherever they went.

- And yet—thousands of years later—their national existence and even their language have been fully restored.

The preservation of the Jews is probably best summed up in Psalm 124, which was originally written in the context of Israel's wilderness wanderings. I think that all who read it will see its modern application:

> What if the LORD had not been on our side?
>   Let all Israel repeat:
> What if the LORD had not been on our side
>   when people attacked us?
> They would have swallowed us alive
>   in their burning anger.
> The waters would have engulfed us;
>   a torrent would have overwhelmed us.
> Yes, the raging waters of their fury
>   would have overwhelmed our very lives.
> Praise the LORD,
>   who did not let their teeth tear us apart!
> We escaped like a bird from a hunter's trap.
>   The trap is broken, and we are free!
> Our help is from the LORD,
>   who made heaven and earth.

The amazing survival of Israel over thousands of years and against all odds has led one Jewish commentator to speculate:

> If the story of Israel were submitted as a movie script, it would be rejected for being too fantastic to believe. After all, the restoration of sovereignty in our ancestral home-land after 2,000 years, the return of the exiles of our people from across the globe, the defense of Israel against implaca-ble enemies, and the transformation of Israel from a desert backwater to a global technological power, seems to defy both history and logic.[16]

Israel's preservation is an incredible thing to ponder!

MAJOR PROPHETIC EVENTS FOR ISRAEL	
Israel was prophesied to be reborn as a nation. This was fulfilled in 1948.	Ezekiel 37
Following Israel's rebirth, Jews were proph-esied to stream back to the Holy Land from every nation in the world. This has been happening yearly since 1948.	Ezekiel 36:24
A military coalition of Russia and Muslim nations will invade Israel. God will destroy the invaders.	Ezekiel 38–39
God watches over Israel, and He will nei-ther slumber nor sleep.	Psalm 121:4
No weapon formed against Israel will prosper.	Isaiah 54:17
A Jewish remnant will convert to Christ at the end of the tribulation period.	Zechariah 12:2–13:1
Israel will experience fulfillment of all cov-enant promises in Christ's millennial kingdom.	Genesis 12:1-3; 15:18-21; 2 Samuel 7:12-13; 22:51

A Northern Military Coalition Will Invade Israel

Some 2600 years ago, Ezekiel prophesied that Israel would be reborn, and that the Jews would regather from nations around the world back to Israel in the end times (Ezekiel 36–37). He then prophesied that, sometime later, there would be an all-out invasion of Israel by a massive northern assault force, with Russia heading up a coalition of Muslim nations. I believe this invasion may take place before the tribulation period.

Ezekiel 38 specifies the identity of these nations:

- *Rosh* refers to modern Russia, to the uttermost north of Israel (Ezekiel 38:2).

- *Magog* refers to the geographical area in the southern part of the former Soviet Union—probably including the former Soviet republics of Kazakhstan, Kyrgyzstan, Uzbekistan, Turkmenistan, Tajikistan, and possibly even northern parts of modern Afghanistan (Ezekiel 38:2).

- *Meshech and Tubal* refers to the geographical territory to the south of the Black and Caspian Seas of Ezekiel's day, which is today modern Turkey (Ezekiel 38:2).

- *Persia* refers to modern Iran. Persia became Iran in 1935 and the Islamic Republic of Iran in 1979 (Ezekiel 38:5).

- *Ethiopia* refers to the geographical territory to the south of Egypt on the Nile River—what is today known as Sudan (Ezekiel 38:5).

- *Put* is a land to the west of Egypt—modern-day Libya. The term may also include the modern countries of Algeria and Tunisia (Ezekiel 38:5).

- *Gomer* is another reference to modern Turkey (Ezekiel 38:6).

- *Beth-togarmah* also refers to modern Turkey, though it may also include Azerbaijan and Armenia (Ezekiel 38:6). (Keep in mind that what today is Turkey was in Bible times divided into smaller territories—Meshech and Tubal, Gomer, and Beth-togarmah.)

The unique alignment of nations described in Ezekiel 38–39 has never occurred in the past but is occurring in modern days. Alliances are already being made among these nations. This lends credence to the idea that we today are living in the end times.

An alliance between these nations may not have made good sense in Ezekiel's day, since they are not near each other geographically. But it makes perfect sense in our day because the nations that make up the coalition—with the exception of Russia—have, since Ezekiel's time, become predominantly Muslim. (Islam emerged in the seventh century AD, and shortly after, many of these Arab territories became Muslim-dominated.) This factor alone is more than enough reason for them to unify in attacking Israel—especially given current Islamic hatred for Israel.

As noted previously, the military head of this massive invading force will be Gog (Ezekiel 38:1). The term *Gog* means "high," "supreme," "a height," or "a high mountain." This czar-like military leader will be a man of great stature who commands tremendous respect.

Though Israel will stand no chance of standing against this massive attack, God will defend His people Israel (Ezekiel 38:17–39:8). He will annihilate Russia and the Muslim invaders. This does not mean that virtually *all* Muslims will be killed. But the Muslim world will be largely decimated following God's wrathful response to the invasion.

Never forget that God has always been the divine protector of Israel. God battles Israel's enemies (Exodus 15:3; Psalm 24:8). Scripture affirms that He who keeps Israel will neither slumber nor sleep (Psalm 121:4). God has promised that no weapon formed against Israel will prosper (Isaiah 54:17). These promises from God are ironclad.

Now, the prophet Ezekiel mentions a precondition for this invasion: Israel must be at peace and "dwell securely" with her geographical neighbors (Ezekiel 38:11). Some believe this peace and security may be rooted in the Abraham Accords Peace Agreement, enacted in September 2020.

The Antichrist Will Head Up a Revived Roman Empire

Meanwhile, a mighty revived Roman Empire will emerge in the end times, and it will be headed by the antichrist. The prophetic book of Daniel in the Old Testament supplies the historical backdrop for the end-times emergence of this empire.

Daniel 7 metaphorically refers to four beasts. These beasts represent successive historical kingdoms that play an essential role in biblical prophecy. The first, Daniel says, was "like a lion with eagles' wings," but "its wings were pulled off" (verse 4). This imagery represents Babylon, its lion-like quality showing power and strength.

Daniel then referred to "a second beast, and it looked like a bear," an animal of great strength (Daniel 7:5; see also 1 Samuel 17:34; Amos 5:19; Hosea 13:8). This kingdom is Medo-Persia and was famous for its strength and fierceness in battle.

The third beast was "like a leopard. It had four bird's wings on its back, and it had four heads. Great authority was given to this beast" (Daniel 7:6). This imagery represents Greece under Alexander the Great, and the "four heads" are the four generals who divided the kingdom following Alexander's death.

The fourth beast was a mongrel beast composed of parts of a lion, bear, and leopard, and was more terrifying and powerful than the three preceding beasts:

> I saw a fourth beast—terrifying, dreadful, and very strong. It devoured and crushed its victims with huge iron teeth and trampled their remains beneath its feet. It was different from any of the other beasts, and it had ten horns.
>
> As I was looking at the horns, suddenly another small horn appeared among them. Three of the first horns were torn out by the roots to make room for it. This little horn had eyes like human eyes and a mouth that was boasting arrogantly.

You may initially scratch your head, wondering what may be meant by such words. In reality, it is not complicated. This imagery refers to the Roman Empire. Rome already existed in ancient days, but it fell apart in the fifth century AD. It will revive, however, in the end times, comprising ten nations ruled by ten kings (ten horns). An eleventh horn—a little horn (the antichrist)—will emerge from within this ten-nation confederacy. The antichrist will start out insignificantly but will grow powerful enough to overtake three of the existing horns (or rulers). He eventually comes into power and dominance over this revived Roman Empire.

We find further details of this revived Roman Empire in Daniel 2 where we read of King Nebuchadnezzar's prophetic dream. In this dream, the end-times Roman Empire is pictured as a mixture of iron and clay (see verses 41-43). Daniel, the great dream-interpreter, saw this as meaning that just as iron is strong, so this latter-day Roman Empire would be strong. But just as iron and clay do not mix, so this latter-day Roman Empire would have some divisions within it. The empire would not be wholly integrated.

THE REVIVED ROMAN EMPIRE	
The antichrist will reign over this empire.	Daniel 2; 7
It will be composed of ten nations.	Daniel 7:7,20
The antichrist will start out insignificantly, but eventually will gain control over the entire empire.	Daniel 7:7-8,24; 2 Thessalonians 2:3-10; Revelation 13:1-10
The empire will be terrifying and powerful.	Daniel 2:40; 7:7
The empire will not be wholly integrated.	Daniel 2:41-43

Rome's Ruler—the Antichrist—Will Sign a Covenant with Israel

Daniel 9:24-27 contains a remarkable prophecy that marks the actual beginning of the tribulation period. The antichrist—the Roman

Empire's leader—will sign a covenant with Israel: "He shall make a strong covenant with many for one week" (Daniel 9:27 ESV). The Holman Christian Standard Bible (HCSB) translates this as a "firm covenant." The Amplified Bible translates it as a "binding and irrevocable covenant."

Such terminology has led some prophecy scholars to conclude that the peace treaty or covenant will enforce an *imposed* peace between Israel and any remaining Muslim peoples. The military might of the revived Roman Empire will enforce the covenant. The idea is, "If you disobey the stipulations of the covenant, you will do so at your own peril."

This means that one geographical area of the world (the revived Roman Empire) will enforce peace in another geographic area of the world (the Middle East). This is apparently one of a number of steps the antichrist will take as he moves toward worldwide dominion. If this is correct, the antichrist's covenant will be unlike previous peace accords, in which various nations voluntarily agreed to peace.

The Jews Will Rebuild a Temple in Jerusalem

Part of the covenant agreement the antichrist will sign with Israel will apparently allow for the rebuilding of the Jewish temple, as well as allow for animal sacrifices within the temple (Daniel 9:27). At the midpoint of the tribulation period, however, the antichrist will disallow any further sacrifices in the temple because he now will seek to be the sole object of worship, claiming to be god on earth.

Jesus, in His Olivet Discourse, warned that the antichrist will then desecrate the Jewish temple. He does this first by sitting inside the temple in the place of God, and then setting up an image of himself within the temple for people to worship (Matthew 24:15).

It is fascinating to see that even today, various Jewish individuals and groups in Jerusalem are working behind the scenes to prepare various materials for the future temple, including priestly robes, temple tapestries, and worship utensils. These items are being prefabricated so that when the Jews finally rebuild the temple, everything will be ready for it. Meanwhile, the newly established Jewish Sanhedrin (religious governing body among the Jews) is raising funds for the rebuilding of the temple and has called for architectural plans to be drawn up. The stage is being set!

A False Religious System Will Emanate from New Babylon During the First Half of the Tribulation Period

References to Babylon in the book of Revelation refer to a revived literal city of Babylon along the Euphrates River—what we might call New Babylon. There are two aspects of New Babylon: (1) The city will promote a false religious system in the first half of the tribulation period; (2) it will become the commercial center of the world in the second half. While there are two different aspects of New Babylon, there is just *one* New Babylon.

Some Bible expositors have suggested that Babylon may be a metaphor perhaps referring to New York City, the United States, Mecca, or some other location. But there are three good reasons Babylon must refer to a literal New Babylon:

1. All the other locations listed in the book of Revelation are literal locations, including the cities of the seven churches in Revelation 2–3.

2. New Babylon is said to be along the Euphrates River in Revelation 9:14 and 16:12. One is unwise to ignore geographical markers.

3. All the other references to Babylon throughout the rest of the Bible *always* point to the godless, sinful, pagan *literal* city of Babylon.[17] That's true about all the mentions of Babylon in the Old Testament. And since the book of Revelation draws heavily from the Old Testament, it is reasonable to infer the term carries the same sense as in the Old Testament.

A literal city of Babylon makes good sense when you think about it. Just as Babylon was the epitome of evil in Old Testament times, so New Babylon will be the epitome of evil in the end times. Just as Babylon promoted false religion in Old Testament times, so New Babylon will promote false religion in the end times. The false religious system associated with New Babylon will dominate during the first half of the tribulation period.

The Big Issues

- Israel lies at the heart and center of Bible prophecy.
- Israel will one day be attacked by a coalition of Russia and Muslim nations. God will destroy the invaders.
- The antichrist—ruler of a revived Roman Empire—will sign and enforce a strong covenant with Israel.
- The Jews will then rebuild their temple in Jerusalem.
- The false religious system promoted by New Babylon will deceive countless people worldwide.

Questions for Reflection

1. Do you agree that events in today's Middle East (Israel and the Muslim nations) have prophetic significance?
2. If yes, are you motivated to make any changes in how you live? Do you feel any sense of urgency in making these changes?

16

WHERE in the World: Part 2

In chapter 15, we began our study of the WHERE of biblical prophecy. We explored prophecies relating to Israel's centrality in Bible prophecy, the coming invasion of Israel by Muslim nations alongside Russia, God's defeat of the invaders, the antichrist's emergence in a revived Roman Empire and his covenant with Israel, and Israel's rebuilding of the temple in Jerusalem.

We will complete our study of the geography of the end times in the present chapter.

A Jewish Remnant Will Escape from Jerusalem After the Antichrist Desecrates the Jewish Temple

Jesus warned in Matthew 24:15-16: "The day is coming when you will see what Daniel the prophet spoke about—the sacrilegious object that causes desecration standing in the Holy Place. (Reader, pay attention!) Then those in Judea must flee to the hills."

The antichrist's desecration of the temple in Jerusalem is often called the "abomination of desolation." In the book of Daniel, such terminology conveys a sense of outrage or horror at the witnessing of a barbaric act of idolatry within God's holy temple. Such acts utterly profane and desecrate the temple (see Daniel 9:27; 11:31; 12:11).

In Daniel 11:31, we read of the antichrist: "His army will take over the Temple fortress, pollute the sanctuary, put a stop to the daily sacrifices, and set up the sacrilegious object that causes desecration." We find further clarity on this "sacrilegious object that causes desecration" in the New Testament. The antichrist's image inside the Jewish temple will amount to an enthronement to deity (see Daniel 9:27; Matthew 24:15). The antichrist will display himself as a god (see Isaiah 14:13-14; Ezekiel 28:2-9). This blasphemous act will desecrate the temple, making it abominable, and therefore desolate. The antichrist will now demand that the world worship and pay idolatrous homage to him. Any who refuse will experience persecution and even martyrdom. The false prophet, who is the antichrist's first lieutenant, will see to this.

When the antichrist claims deity, things turn south rapidly for the Jews living in Jerusalem. Jesus thus warned in Matthew 24:16-21:

> "Those in Judea must flee to the hills. A person out on the deck of a roof must not go down into the house to pack. A person out in the field must not return even to get a coat. How terrible it will be for pregnant women and for nursing mothers in those days. And pray that your flight will not be in winter or on the Sabbath. For there will be greater anguish than at any time since the world began. And it will never be so great again."

Here is what it comes down to: When these horrific circumstances unfold in Jerusalem, Jesus urges the Jews living there to forget about personal belongings and rocket out of town. Time spent gathering things might mean the difference between life and death. From this point onward, the distress for Jewish people will escalate dramatically (see Jeremiah 30:7).

A Jewish Remnant Will Find Refuge in the Wilderness

With the Jews exiting Jerusalem, they need someplace to go. Revelation 12 speaks of God's providential relocation of the Jewish remnant in the wilderness: "She [Israel] was given two wings like those of a great eagle so she could fly to the place prepared for her in the wilderness" (verse 14).

Wings often represent protection and deliverance in the Bible (see Psalm 91:4; Isaiah 40:31). For example, in the Exodus account, when God delivered the Jews from Egyptian bondage, He said, "You have seen what I did to the Egyptians. You know how I carried you on eagles' wings and brought you to myself" (Exodus 19:4). Hence, the "two wings" in Revelation 12:14 point to God's supernatural and providential delivering power.

Scripture does not identify the hiding place in the wilderness. A number of Bible expositors, however, believe the Jews may find refuge in Bozrah/Petra, about eighty miles south of Jerusalem. The natural terrain in this area is favorable for caring for multiple thousands of people.

Scripture informs us that God will preserve the Jewish remnant for "a time, times, and half a time." This refers to the last three-and-a-half years of the tribulation period (see Daniel 7:25; 12:7). This period also coincides with the forty-two months referenced in Revelation 11:2 and 13:5. Scripture designates the last three-and-a-half years of the tribulation period as the "great tribulation," so horrible will things be. This makes God's protection of the remnant all the more important.

GOD'S PROTECTION OF HIS PEOPLE	
God is our hiding place.	Psalm 32:7
God is our refuge.	Deuteronomy 33:27; Psalm 27:5; 31:20; 46:1
God is our rock and fortress.	Psalm 71:3; Proverbs 14:26
God protects us from the plots of the wicked.	Psalm 64:2; 119:154; 140:1
We dwell in the secret place of the Most High.	Psalm 91:1
God delivers us out of trouble.	Psalm 34:17-19; 121:8
When we pass through deep waters, God will be there.	Isaiah 43:2

The Antichrist's Reach Will Expand Globally

The antichrist will one day explode into global dominion. He will rule the entire world, not just the revived Roman Empire. The book of Revelation assures us that eventually during the tribulation period, "the whole world" will give "allegiance to the beast" (Revelation 13:3). The antichrist "was given authority to rule over every tribe and people and language and nation. And all the people who belong to this world worshiped the beast" (verses 7-8). We are also told that the false prophet "required all the earth and its people to worship the first beast" (verse 12). This is where the infamous "mark of the beast" comes into the picture. Revelation 13:16-17 tells us that the false prophet "required everyone—small and great, rich and poor, free and slave—to be given a mark on the right hand or the forehead. And no one could buy or sell anything without that mark, which was either the name of the beast or the number representing his name." There will now be a globalized *political* union, *religious* union, and *economic* union. All will be "one"— and all will be controlled by the antichrist.

When one considers the multiple cascading problems now facing humanity—including the Middle East conflict, terrorism, overpopulation, starvation, pollution, famine, national and international crime, cyberwarfare, economic instability, and widespread illness such as that caused by the COVID-19 pandemic—it is entirely feasible that increasing numbers of people will come to believe that such problems can be solved only on a global level. They may think the only hope for human survival is a strong and effective world government. People may yearn for a powerful leader who can chart a clear global course toward stability. Such a leader is indeed coming, and he may already be alive in the world. Scripture identifies him as the antichrist. He will eventually be viewed as "god on earth" by people worldwide.

The technology that makes possible a world government— including instant global media via television and radio, cyberspace, and supercomputers—is now in place. Technology has greased the skids for the emergence of globalism in our day.

ANTI-GOD GLOBALISM	
Whole world will give allegiance to the antichrist	Revelation 13:3
Antichrist will rule over all people	Revelation 13:7-8
Antichrist will be worshipped by all people	Revelation 13:7-8,12
Antichrist will control the economy of the entire world	Revelation 13:16-17
Antichrist will head a global anti-God union	Revelation 13:3-18

New Babylon Will Transform into the Commercial Center of the World

New Babylon will promote a false religious system during the first half of the tribulation period. This might be some kind of a religious amalgamation that will pull together people of various religious backgrounds into one great ecclesiastical alliance—an extremely broad "world church."

Revelation 17:16 reveals that the antichrist will initially use this false religious system to bring unity to the peoples of the world. Once he has accomplished this purpose, he will no longer need the false religion. He will dispose of it with the help of his ten sub-commanders at the midpoint of the tribulation period. He will now seek to become the sole object of worship as "god on earth" (Daniel 11:36-38; 2 Thessalonians 2:4; Revelation 13:8,15). No competing religious systems will be permitted.

New Babylon will now transform into the commercial center of the world. Revelation 18 supplies some important facts about commercial New Babylon:

1. The political leaders of the world will play a pivotal role in the global influence and affluence of New Babylon. Their motivation is personal wealth. They will all get rich off of New Babylon.

2. Businesspeople from around the world will also grow rich because of their association with New Babylon.

3. New Babylon will purchase a wide array of products from all over the world.

4. New Babylon will be headed up by an economic genius—the Satan-inspired antichrist.

5. The mark of the beast will be directly connected to New Babylon's success. After all, no one can buy or sell anything without receiving the mark (Revelation 13:16-17). We deduce that the products purchased by New Babylon will be from merchants who have received the mark of the beast.

6. New Babylon will thrive throughout the second half of the tribulation period.

Armageddon Will Erupt at the Mount of Megiddo at the End of the Tribulation Period

Armageddon will be a catastrophic war campaign that will take place at the very end of the tribulation period (Daniel 11:40-45; Joel 3:9-17; Zechariah 14:1-3; Revelation 16:14-16). The word *Armageddon* means "Mount of Megiddo," and refers to a location about sixty miles north of Jerusalem. This is the location of Barak's battle with the Canaanites (Judges 4) and Gideon's battle with the Midianites (Judges 7). This will be the site for the outbreak of Armageddon—the final horrific battle of humankind just before the second coming of Jesus Christ (Revelation 16:16).

Napoleon once commented that this site is perhaps the greatest battlefield he had ever witnessed. Of course, the battles Napoleon fought will dim in comparison to Armageddon. So horrible will Armageddon be that no one would survive if it were not for Christ coming again (Matthew 24:22).

There are eight phases of Armageddon, and they involve different geographical areas:

Phase 1: The allied armies of the antichrist will gather at the Mount of Megiddo to initiate the final destruction of the Jews (Revelation 16:12-16).

Phase 2: Meanwhile, God will destroy New Babylon (Revelation 18).

Phase 3: The antichrist will attack and destroy Jerusalem (Zechariah 12:1-3; 14:1-2).

Phase 4: The antichrist will move against the remnant of Jews in the wilderness, probably in Bozrah/Petra, about eighty miles south of Jerusalem (see Matthew 24:16-31; Revelation 12:6).

Phase 5: Endangered by the forces of the antichrist, the remnant of Jews in the wilderness will convert to Christ. God will remove their spiritual blindness. Under the urging of the Jewish leaders, the Jews in the remnant will confess their sins and believe in Jesus for salvation (Hosea 6:1-3; Joel 2:28-29; Zechariah 12:2–13:1). They will plead for their newly found Messiah to return and deliver them.

Phase 6: Jesus will personally return to rescue the Jewish remnant (Acts 1:9-11; Matthew 24:30; Revelation 1:7).

Phase 7: Jesus will confront the forces of the antichrist and slay them with the word of His mouth (Revelation 19:11-21).

Phase 8: Jesus will victoriously ascend the Mount of Olives, not far from Jerusalem (Zechariah 14:3-4). When He does this, cataclysmic events occur that bring an end to the tribulation period. These include:

- An earthquake of globally staggering proportions. The topography of the earth will drastically alter.

- Jerusalem will split into three areas.

- The Mount of Olives will split into two parts, creating a valley.

- There will be a horrific hailstorm, and the sun and moon will darken.

- As these horrific events subside, the tribulation period finally comes to a close.

Lessons Learned from the Seven Churches of Asia Minor

In Revelation 2–3, we read about seven churches in seven cities in Asia Minor—Ephesus, Smyrna, Pergamum, Thyatira, Sardis, Philadelphia, and Laodicea. The apostle John was a spiritual overseer of all seven churches. He was literally their spiritual father.

While these chapters do not speak of the distant prophetic future, they are nevertheless contained in a prophetic book (Revelation), and for good reason. There are powerful spiritual lessons we can sift from an examination of these churches—lessons that are especially important as we move further into the end times. Among them:

- Doctrinal accuracy and moral purity are important, but these things are not enough. Supreme love for God and others is also necessary. Christianity is more than just being doctrinally correct. It involves an ongoing love relationship with the Lord.

- Do not sweat over earthly troubles. Our destiny in heaven is secure. Rejoice!

- Repent of openness to false teachings, which can lead to inappropriate behavior.

- Abstain from all forms of fornication.

- Avoid hypocrisy, which involves the pretense of having a virtuous character when in reality no such virtue is present.

- Do not be lukewarm in your commitment to God.

The Big Ideas

- A Jewish remnant will escape Jerusalem following the antichrist's desecration of the Jewish temple.

- Under God's providence, the Jewish remnant will relocate in the wilderness, probably in the Bozrah/Petra area far south of Jerusalem.

- The antichrist will rise to global dominion.

- New Babylon will become the commercial center of the world.

- Armageddon will erupt at the Mount of Megiddo at the end of the tribulation period.

- Jerusalem will be destroyed, and the Jewish remnant will become endangered in the Bozrah/Petra area.

- We learn good lessons on how to live in the end times from Christ's words to the seven churches in Revelation 2–3.

Questions for Reflection

1. Just as Christ knows all that goes on in churches, so He knows all that goes on in each of our lives. Does that reality comfort you or scare you?

2. Do you ever struggle with hypocrisy in your Christian life? How so? What can you do about it?

3. Do you ever sense your relationship with God is lukewarm? How so? What can you do about it?

PART 5

WHY DOES GOD GIVE US PROPHECIES OF THE END TIMES?

17

A Motivation to Live Expectantly

We have gone on quite a journey together in this book. So far we've examined the WHO, WHAT, WHEN, and WHERE of Bible prophecy. We now shift our attention to the final section of the book—the WHY of Bible prophecy. More specifically, *Why does God give us prophecies of the end times?*

I believe there are three primary answers to this question: God gives us end-time prophecies to (1) motivate us to live expectantly, (2) motivate us to live righteously, and (3) motivate us to live with an eternal perspective. Each of these is important, and I will devote an entire chapter to each as we explore what Scripture says about them.

Many prophecies addressed in this book could potentially fuel our sense of expectancy for the future. But three are especially relevant: (1) the rapture is imminent; (2) we will be with Christ following the moment of death; and (3) our raptured or resurrected bodies will be awesome.

The Rapture Is Imminent

The term *imminent* means "ready to take place" or "impending." The apostle Paul tells us that "time is running out" and "our salvation is nearer now than when we first believed" because the rapture is imminent (Romans 13:11-12). It could happen at any moment. At the end of each day, the Christian is that much closer to the rapture.

Understandably, Paul exults that we "eagerly wait" for the Lord Jesus Christ (1 Corinthians 1:7; Philippians 3:20; see also Hebrews 9:28). After all, "the Lord is coming soon" (Philippians 4:5). We "are looking forward to the coming of God's Son from heaven" (1 Thessalonians 1:10). We live in *expectancy* of the rapture.

Keep in mind that the rapture is a signless event. There are no prophecies awaiting fulfillment before it occurs. This is in contrast to the second coming of Christ, which has seven years of prophetic signs preceding it during the tribulation period (Revelation 4–18).

We Will Be with Christ Following the Moment of Death

What if we die before the rapture? No problem! Following the moment of death, we will go directly into the presence of the Lord Jesus in heaven.

The scriptural backdrop is that you and I have both a material and an immaterial nature or aspect. The material part of a human being is the body (see Genesis 2:7; 3:19). The immaterial part is the soul or spirit. The words *soul* and *spirit* are interchangeable in Scripture. Scripture refers to a person's entire immaterial part as "soul" in 1 Peter 2:11 and "spirit" in James 2:26 (ESV). We conclude they are identical.

This helps us to understand better what happens at the moment of death. At death, the spirit (or soul) slips out of the physical body just as easily as a hand slips out of a glove (see Genesis 35:18; 2 Corinthians 5:8; Philippians 1:21-23). When this happens, the "clothing" of the body is no longer on the spirit, so we experience a sense of "nakedness" (2 Corinthians 5:1-4). (Don't worry—this sense of nakedness is only temporary. We'll eventually receive resurrection bodies.)

Many Scripture verses speak of the spirit departing from the body at death. Ecclesiastes 12:7, for example, tells us that at the moment of death, "the spirit will return to God who gave it." Jesus experienced this following His death on the cross. Right before He died, He prayed to the heavenly Father: "Father, I entrust my spirit into your hands" (Luke 23:46). Jesus knew that His physical body was about to die. He knew that once He died, His spirit would depart the body. It is this spirit that He entrusted to the Father's safekeeping.

Stephen is another example. He was a firm believer in the Lord Jesus Christ. Even at the threat of death, he would not deny his Lord.

Some Jewish antagonists threw stones at him to kill him. Right before he died, he prayed, "Lord Jesus, receive my spirit" (Acts 7:59). Stephen knew his physical body was about to die. But he also knew that his spirit would survive death, departing from the body at that very moment. He promptly committed his spirit into the safekeeping of Jesus.

Because the spirit departs the body and goes to be with the Lord at death, the apostle Paul affirmed he had no fear of death: "We are fully confident, and we would rather be away from these earthly bodies, for then we will be at home with the Lord" (2 Corinthians 5:8).

Paul also exulted: "My desire is to depart and be with Christ, for that is far better" (Philippians 1:23 esv). The word translated "depart" is rich in the original Greek, indicating freedom from chains. Here on earth, we are chained or anchored to the hardships and heartaches of this life. At death, however, these chains break. We are set free for entry into heaven. At the moment of death, the spirit departs the physical body and goes directly into the presence of the Lord.

Death for the Christian is simply a gateway into paradise (or heaven). Recall that during his ministry, the apostle Paul was "caught up to the third heaven," also called "paradise" (2 Corinthians 12:2-3). Paul had no fear of death. He knew where he was going!

The word *paradise* literally means "garden of pleasure" or "garden of delight." While Paul was there, he "heard things so astounding that they cannot be expressed in words, things no human is allowed to tell." This paradise of God is apparently so resplendently glorious, so wondrous, that God forbade Paul to say anything about it to those still in the earthly realm. Maybe this explains why Paul so desired to get back there (Philippians 1:21-23). And perhaps this explains why Paul affirmed that "no eye has seen, no ear has heard, and no mind has imagined what God has prepared for those who love him" (1 Corinthians 2:9). Paul was a firsthand eyewitness of heaven. He saw with his own eyes that paradise is indescribably glorious.

This means we can live with a strong sense of expectancy.

OUR HEAVENLY HABITAT		
Description	Scripture	Meaning
Heavenly Country	Hebrews 11:13-15	A country full of light, glory, splendor, and love
Holy City	Revelation 21:1-2	A city of purity, with no sin
Home of Righteousness	2 Peter 3:13	A perfect environment of righteousness
Kingdom of Light	Colossians 1:12	A kingdom of Christ, who is the light of the world (John 8:12)
Paradise of God	Revelation 2:7	A garden of pleasure and delight
New Jerusalem	Revelation 21:12-14	The capital city of heaven

We Will Be Resurrected with Awesome Bodies

The apostle Paul describes the death of our mortal bodies and our subsequent resurrection with an incredible word picture: "Our earthly bodies are planted in the ground when we die, but they will be raised to live forever. Our bodies are buried in brokenness, but they will be raised in glory. They are buried in weakness, but they will be raised in strength" (1 Corinthians 15:42-43).

Think about these words. Just as one sows a seed in the ground, so the mortal body is sown in the sense of burial in the ground. Following the burial, our bodies decompose and return to dust. But that is not the end of the story. Our bodies will one day experience physical resurrection!

Paul says our present bodies are "broken." They succumb to disease and death. As we live year to year, we continuously struggle to fight off dangerous infections. We do everything we can to stay healthy, but we inevitably get sick. Worse yet, we all eventually die. It is just a matter of time.

Our body upgrades, however, will be glorious and imperishable.

This means that all liability to disease and death will vanish. Never again will we have to worry about infections or passing away.

Paul then reaffirms the same thing in another way. He says our present mortal bodies succumb to "weakness." As time passes, vitality decreases, illness comes, and old age follows with its wrinkles and decrepitude. Eventually, in old age, we may become utterly incapacitated, not able to move around and do the simplest of tasks. Again, however, this is not the end of the story.

Our dead bodies "will be raised in strength." They will never again be subject to aging, decay, or death. Our new bodies will be energetic. We will never again have to lament, "I'm too tired." We will be able to walk and jump with vitality. Our health and strength will never deteriorate or wane.

Words seem inadequate to describe the differences between our present frail bodies and our future resurrection bodies. There will be no more cholesterol buildup, no more heart disease, no more kidney failure, no more diabetes, no more blindness or deafness, and no more aging of the skin with its wrinkles. We will enjoy perpetual youth with a fullness of vitality and energy. It will be awesome!

Of course, some Christians will bypass death altogether. If we happen to be alive on the earth at the moment of the rapture, our earthly bodies will be instantly transformed into glorified bodies. Either way—whether we are resurrected or instantly transformed at the rapture—we will all have awesome bodies.

The Glorified Body—Sturdy as a Building

The apostle Paul compares our earthly bodies to tents and our permanent glorified bodies to buildings (2 Corinthians 5:1-4). He was speaking in terms his listeners would understand.

The Jews of Paul's day knew that the temporary tabernacle of Israel's wanderings in the wilderness was a giant tent-like structure. They also knew that a glorious permanent building—the stone temple—soon took its place when Israel entered the promised land.

Paul uses this contrast between the temporary tabernacle and the stone temple to represent the substantial contrast between our present mortal bodies and our future glorified bodies. If Paul were speaking to people in our modern world, he would likely contrast a high-rise building with a small pup tent.

The temporary "tent" (or body) in which believers now dwell will one day fall in death. In its place will be an eternal, immortal, imperishable body that Paul compares to a sturdy building (see 1 Corinthians 15:42,53-54). Is this not a good cause to rejoice? We can live with a high sense of expectancy. The blessings awaiting us in heaven are unfathomable.

The Big Ideas

We can live with a strong sense of expectancy because...

- the rapture is imminent
- we will be with Christ following the moment of death
- we will one day receive awesome glorified bodies

Questions for Reflection

1. Do you struggle with any persistent physical ailments? Do you ever feel like your "tent" is wearing down? How does it make you feel to know that your glorified body will be characterized by perpetual strength, health, and youth?

2. What most excites you about what awaits you in the afterlife?

18

A Motivation to Live Righteously

In the previous chapter I noted that one WHY for God's gift of biblical prophecy is to fuel our sense of expectancy for the future. Another WHY relates to how prophecy can motivate us to pursue righteousness and purity in our daily lives.

Many prophetic Bible verses follow with an appeal to personal purity. This means that as we study prophecy, it ought to change the way we live. It ought to influence our behavior. The best illustrations of this are found in the writings of Paul, Peter, John, and Daniel.

Wisdom from Paul

The apostle Paul shows the close connection between prophecy and purity in Romans 13:11-14:

> This is all the more urgent, for you know how late it is; time is running out. Wake up, for our salvation is nearer now than when we first believed. The night is almost gone; the day of salvation will soon be here. So remove your dark deeds like dirty clothes, and put on the shining armor of right living. Because we belong to the day, we must live decent lives for all to see. Don't participate in the darkness of wild parties and drunkenness, or in sexual promiscuity and immoral living, or in quarreling and jealousy. Instead, clothe yourself with the presence of the Lord Jesus Christ. And don't let yourself think about ways to indulge your evil desires.

Paul is apparently speaking of the rapture of the church in this passage. He says that because the rapture is imminent—because it could happen *at any moment*—we ought to clean up our lives and pursue righteousness. Get rid of all sin and "clothe yourself with the presence of the Lord Jesus Christ." *Live your life as if the rapture could happen today!*

Wisdom from Peter

Peter also points to the close connection between prophecy and purity. He speaks of the necessity of prayer, being loving, sharing shelter and food, and using our spiritual gifts in serving others—all in view of the nearing prophetic future:

> The end of the world is coming soon. Therefore, be earnest and disciplined in your prayers. Most important of all, continue to show deep love for each other, for love covers a multitude of sins. Cheerfully share your home with those who need a meal or a place to stay.
>
> God has given each of you a gift from his great variety of spiritual gifts. Use them well to serve one another (1 Peter 4:7-10).

Later, in 2 Peter 3:10-14, Peter likewise exhorts us:

> The day of the Lord will come as unexpectedly as a thief. Then the heavens will pass away with a terrible noise, and the very elements themselves will disappear in fire, and the earth and everything on it will be found to deserve judgment.
>
> Since everything around us is going to be destroyed like this, what holy and godly lives you should live, looking forward to the day of God and hurrying it along. On that day, he will set the heavens on fire, and the elements will melt away in the flames. But we are looking forward to the new heavens and new earth he has promised, a world filled with God's righteousness.
>
> And so, dear friends, while you are waiting for these things to happen, make every effort to be found living peaceful lives that are pure and blameless in his sight.

In this latter passage, Peter provides a panoramic sweep spanning from the day of the Lord (which includes the tribulation period) through the eventual establishment of the new heavens and new earth. Because of the glorious future that lies ahead for Christians, "what holy and godly lives you should live," Peter says. We should live lives "that are pure and blameless in his sight."

Wisdom from John

John, too, points to the close connection between prophecy and purity. In 1 John 3:2-3, he affirms:

> Dear friends, we are already God's children, but he has not yet shown us what we will be like when Christ appears. But we do know that we will be like him, for we will see him as he really is. And all who have this eager expectation will keep themselves pure, just as he is pure.

The appearance of Christ that John speaks of pertains to the future rapture. What a glorious day that will be! My prophecy mentor at Dallas Theological Seminary, the late John F. Walvoord, commented that "the hope of the rapture, when we will meet the Savior, should be a sanctifying force in our lives. We will be made completely like Him then; so we should endeavor with His help to serve Him faithfully now and to lead lives of purity."[18] We should take advantage of every moment to live for the Lord with gusto. We should use our time wisely.

USING TIME WISELY
"Be careful how you live. Don't live like fools, but like those who are wise. Make the most of every opportunity in these evil days" (Ephesians 5:15-17).
"Live wisely among those who are not believers, and make the most of every opportunity" (Colossians 4:5).
"Teach us to realize the brevity of life, so that we may grow in wisdom" (Psalm 90:12).
"Lord, remind me how brief my time on earth will be. Remind me that my days are numbered—how fleeting my life is" (Psalm 39:4).

Wisdom from Daniel

Daniel wrote the biblical book that bears his name (see Daniel 8:15,27; 9:2; 10:2,7; 12:4-5). His book reveals God's prophetic plan for both the Gentiles (2–7) and Israel (8–12). In the process, Daniel addresses the future revived Roman Empire, the antichrist who will reign over this empire, the antichrist's defilement of the future Jewish temple during the tribulation period, the antichrist's persecution of the Jews, and much more. Daniel's mind was brimming with revelations from God about the prophetic future.

It is fascinating to observe how Daniel lived in view of the prophetic revelations given to him. Daniel is an example of how *you and I* ought to live in light of prophecy.

Obedience. Daniel consistently maintained obedience to God. For instance, after King Darius banned prayer to any god but himself for thirty days, Daniel's first act was to go home and pray to the one true God, instead of praying to Darius. For this, the king had Daniel thrown into the lions' den. But God honored Daniel's act of obedience by rescuing him from the lions (Daniel 6).

We find another example in Daniel's three Hebrew friends. Nebuchadnezzar commanded that they bow down and worship his golden image. They refused. They knew that to engage in this act would be idolatrous and bring offense to the one true God. Because of their refusal, the king sentenced the three Hebrew youths to be thrown into a fiery furnace. But God honored their act of obedience by rescuing them in that furnace (Daniel 3).

Daniel and his friends obeyed God, *no matter what!* I hate to say it, but many modern Christians seem to obey God only when it is convenient. When it's not convenient, they lapse.

How we need to mimic Daniel and his friends! If Christians could only grasp that obedience to God is in their best interests, perhaps they would be sufficiently motivated to obey God moment by moment, day by day. Scripture reveals that obeying God brings...

- blessing (Luke 11:28)
- long life (1 Kings 3:14; John 8:51)

- happiness (Psalm 112:1; 119:56)

- peace (Proverbs 1:33)

- well-being (Jeremiah 7:23; see also Exodus 19:5; Leviticus 26:3-4; Deuteronomy 4:40; 12:28; 28:1; Joshua 1:8; 1 Chronicles 22:13; Isaiah 1:19)

Walking by faith. Another trait we see in Daniel is that he always walked by faith and not by sight. The king had Daniel tossed into a lions' den. From a "walking by sight" perspective, death was certain. But Daniel maintained faith, and God rewarded that faith by rescuing him from the lions (Daniel 6).

The same is true of Daniel's three Hebrew friends. From a "walking by sight" perspective, being tossed into a fiery furnace is a sure death sentence. But they maintained faith, and God delivered them from the fire (Daniel 3).

As we move further into the end times, let's follow Daniel's example by walking by faith and not by sight. The following verses will help you: Psalm 40:4; 118:8; Proverbs 3:5; Jeremiah 17:7; Matthew 15:28; 21:21-22; Luke 17:5-6; Romans 10:17; 2 Corinthians 5:7; 1 Timothy 1:19; Hebrews 10:35; 11:1; 1 Peter 1:7.

A good reputation. Daniel consistently sought to keep a good reputation, even among pagans. Daniel's stellar reputation began in the first year of his captivity and lasted all the way to his death. His excellent reputation not only brought him before kings but also brought him great honor and exaltation throughout life. As we continue to live in the last days, let's resolve to follow Daniel's example and pursue a good reputation among all people (1 Samuel 2:1-5; 29:3; Psalm 86:2; 87:3; 109:4; Proverbs 22:1; Acts 17:11).

Integrity. Perhaps the most notable character trait of Daniel is that he was consistently a man of integrity (Daniel 1:7-9; 6:10). This integrity was clear to all who encountered him—including King Nebuchadnezzar and King Darius. Daniel would have agreed with Paul's words in 2 Corinthians 8:21: "We are careful to be honorable before the Lord, but we also want everyone else to see that we are honorable."

We all ought to follow Daniel's example in living as people of integrity, especially in view of the end times. Following are some verses that can help you in this regard: Proverbs 11:3; 19:1; 20:7; 28:6; Psalm 25:21; 26:1; Micah 6:8; Acts 24:16; Titus 2:1-14; Hebrews 13:18; and James 1:22-25.

Humility. Finally, Daniel set a great example of humility. He was a humble man who consistently pointed away from his own abilities and instead toward God (Daniel 2:27-28). He had the same humble attitude as John the Baptist, who said of Jesus, "He must become greater and greater, and I must become less and less" (John 3:30).

Daniel knew that those who want to please God must walk in humility. God exalts the humble: "Humble yourselves before the Lord, and he will lift you up in honor" (James 4:10; see also Proverbs 15:33; 22:4; 29:23; Luke 1:52; 1 Peter 5:5-6). Daniel humbled himself throughout his life, and God consistently exalted and honored him. You and I ought to follow Daniel's example.

Maintaining Christian Unity

I close this chapter with a brief exhortation to Christian unity. Even though Christians love to debate many of the finer points relating to Bible prophecy, they agree on the big stuff:

- Christ is coming again.
- Christians will receive incredible body upgrades (resurrection bodies).
- Christians will be held accountable at a future judgment for how they lived on earth.
- Christians will live forever with God face-to-face.
- One day there will be no more sin, suffering, Satan, or death.

Isn't all this great news? Despite all the differences Christians may have on the finer points of prophecy, we ought to keep the big stuff at the forefront of our thinking.

And whenever we debate the finer points of biblical prophecy, we need to avoid divisive attitudes. I think we all need a good dose of humility (modeled by Daniel) to temper our leanings toward dogmatism.

We should all feel free to hold our own cherished views on the specific issues of Bible prophecy and even to become fully convinced that we are right. But we should never make these nonessential teachings tests of orthodoxy or Christian fellowship. As a pretrib (who believes the rapture will occur before the tribulation period), I have plenty of posttrib friends—and I intend to keep it that way.

It is not merely *what we believe* but also *how we behave* that is important. Jesus emphasized the importance of truth. He said, "You will know the truth, and the truth will set you free" (John 8:32). But He also said that *love*, not merely *truth*, is the distinguishing mark of a Christian (John 13:35). One can be right in what he says and wrong in the way he says it. The true Christian should strive to be as helpful and loving as he is correct. The apostle Paul struck the perfect balance when he exhorted the Ephesians to "speak the truth in love" (Ephesians 4:15).

Debate, yes!

Divide, no!

The Big Ideas

- Bible prophecy should serve as a strong motivation to live righteously and in purity, as taught in the writings of Paul, Peter, and John.

- As we continue to move deeper into the last days, let us mimic Daniel in obedience to God, walking by faith, keeping a good reputation, living in integrity, and staying humble.

- It's okay if some Christians disagree with us on some of the finer points of Bible prophecy. After all, we agree on all the big stuff.

Questions for Reflection

1. Can you summarize what you've learned in this chapter in a single sentence that you can use as a life principle?

2. What impresses you most about how Daniel lived in light of the prophetic future?

19

A Motivation to Live with an Eternal Perspective

Bible prophecy can motivate us to live expectantly and to live righteously. It can also motivate us to live with an eternal perspective. An eternal perspective, as I understand it, involves keeping our eyes on heaven, staying aware of our mortality, and resolving to live in light of eternal realities.

Keep Your Eyes on Heaven

Many prophecies in the Bible relate to heaven. God provides these prophecies not just so we can learn about our eternal home. He also provides them to get us excited while we yet live on the earth.

One of my all-time favorite Bible passages is Colossians 3:1-2: "Since you have been raised to new life with Christ, set your sights on the realities of heaven, where Christ sits in the place of honor at God's right hand. Think about the things of heaven, not the things of earth."

As great as this passage is in English, it is even richer—and far more intense—in the original Greek. It communicates the idea, "Diligently, actively, single-mindedly think on the realities of heaven."

It is also a present tense in the Greek. This conveys *continuous action*. The verse communicates the idea, "Perpetually keep on thinking about the realities of heaven. Make it an ongoing process."

Putting our insights together in an enhanced translation, we might render the central part of the passage this way: "Perpetually keep on thinking about the realities of heaven in a diligent, active, and singled-minded way. Do not let up. Work hard to keep heaven at the forefront of your thoughts."

Let us not forget that "we are citizens of heaven, where the Lord Jesus Christ lives. And we are eagerly waiting for him to return as our Savior" (Philippians 3:20). Heaven is our real home (John 14:2-3). Our names are registered there (Luke 10:20). An inheritance awaits us there (1 Peter 1:4). Our Christian loved ones who have already passed over also await us there (Hebrews 12:23). All of this is part and parcel of our eternal perspective.

It is no wonder that Hebrews 11:13 says God's people are but "foreigners and nomads here on earth." We are all pilgrims en route to a better country—a heavenly one (Hebrews 11:16).

Through the years, I have enjoyed reading various books on the Puritans. J.I. Packer has done a great deal of research on them, and he notes that they saw themselves as "God's pilgrims, traveling home through rough country; God's warriors, battling the world, the flesh, and the devil; and God's servants, under orders to worship, fellowship, and do all the good they could as they went along."[19] Such words seem foreign to modern Christianity, and to our detriment. I, for one, think the Puritans were right.

Based on what he has learned about the Puritans, Packer affirms that the "lack of long, strong thinking about our promised hope of glory is a major cause of our plodding, lackluster lifestyle." He notes that "it is the heavenly Christian that is the lively Christian." The Puritans understood that we "run so slowly, and strive so lazily, because we so little mind the prize…So let Christians animate themselves daily to run the race set before them by practicing heavenly meditation."[20]

One Puritan Packer talks about is Richard Baxter, whose recommended daily habit was to "dwell on the glory of the heavenly life to which one was going." Baxter daily practiced "holding heaven at the forefront of his thoughts and desires." The hope of heaven brought him joy, and that joy brought him strength. Baxter once said, "A heavenly mind is a joyful mind; this is the nearest and truest way to live a life of comfort…A heart in heaven will be a most excellent preservative against temptations, a powerful means to kill thy corruptions."[21]

DESCRIPTIONS OF HEAVEN	
It is a heavenly country, filled with light, glory, and love.	Hebrews 11:13-15
It is a holy city, full of purity and without sin.	Revelation 21:1-2
It is the home of righteousness.	2 Peter 3:13
It is a kingdom of light, where Christ—the light of the world—dwells.	John 8:12; Colossians 1:12
It is the paradise of God, full of pleasure and delight.	Revelation 2:7
The New Jerusalem is there—a celestial city in heaven that will be our eternal dwelling place.	Revelation 21

Stay Aware of Your Mortality

The older I get, the more important I think it is to ponder heaven because life on earth is so short. It seems like I blink three times, and three decades have passed. Where do the years go?

My mind still feels young. But when I look in the mirror I am once again reminded that I am aging. I see the same in all my friends and acquaintances. We are all getting older, and to some it may seem like death is just around the corner.

Philip Yancey once said our time on earth amounts to a mere "dot in eternity."[22] This dot in eternity is quickly passing away. It will soon be over. Whether we realize it or not, we are all literally hurling into eternity at a dizzying pace.

I am not trying to be morbid. Part of keeping an eternal perspective is a constant awareness of our mortality. We each ought to pray with the psalmist,

> Teach us to realize the brevity of life,
> so that we may grow in wisdom.
> (Psalm 90:12)

"Lord, remind me how brief my time on earth will be.
  Remind me that my days are numbered—
  how fleeting my life is."
                                    (Psalm 39:4)

Christians who wisely ponder their mortality are most often the ones who keep the eternal perspective described in Colossians 3:1-2.

It also seems to me that the older we get, the more force Ecclesiastes 3:11 has: God "has planted eternity in the human heart." Though we live in a world of passing time, we have intimations of eternity within our hearts. We instinctively think of *forever*. We seem to intrinsically realize that beyond this life lies the possibility of a shoreless ocean of time. It is wondrous to even ponder it. We are heaven-bent; our hearts have an inner tilt upward.

Once we have arrived in heaven, we will live forever in a pain-free, age-free, and death-free environment. Looking back, our life on earth will seem like a brief moment in time. John Wenham once commented that "not only is it certain that this life will end, but it is certain that from the perspective of eternity it will be seen to have passed in a flash."[23]

I am not the only one who feels this way. From the first book in the Bible to the last, we read of great men and women of God who gave evidence that eternity permeated their hearts. We read of people like Abel, Enoch, Noah, Abraham, and David—each yearning to live with God in eternity. They were each "looking forward to a country they can call their own. If they had longed for the country they came from, they could have gone back. But they were looking for a better place, a heavenly homeland. That is why God is not ashamed to be called their God, for he has prepared a city for them" (Hebrews 11:14-16). That city is in heaven—the New Jerusalem (Revelation 21:10-21).

When I read the psalms, I often reflect on heavenly realities and the yearning in the human heart for the eternal. Psalm 42:1-2 is one of my favorites:

As the deer longs for streams of water,
  so I long for you, O God.

I thirst for God, the living God.
When can I go and stand before him?

I will be able to "stand before him" following the moment of my death or following the rapture, whichever comes first. I love the way David put it: "I will live in the house of the LORD forever" (Psalm 23:6).

YEARNING FOR THE AFTERLIFE	
"We would rather be away from these earthly bodies, for then we will be at home with the Lord."	2 Corinthians 5:8
"I long to go and be with Christ, which would be far better for me."	Philippians 1:23
"In your presence there is fullness of joy; at your right hand are pleasures forevermore."	Psalm 16:11 ESV

Resolving to Live in Light of Eternal Realities

As you ponder the reality that God "has planted eternity in the human heart" (Ecclesiastes 3:11), what does your heart tell you at this moment about the direction your life should take—in terms of how you live day to day—from this moment onward? It is a question worthy of deepest reflection.

Whenever I speak to others about heavenly realities and an eternal perspective, I always point to the great revivalist preacher, philosopher, and theologian Jonathan Edwards. Edwards lived from 1703 to 1758 and was in the Puritan habit of framing spiritual resolutions to discipline himself in his Christian walk. In several resolutions, he reminded himself to ponder the reality that he would one day die. He also pondered how he should live if he knew he had only an hour left before passing through death's door. In his thinking, his life was a step-by-step journey toward heaven—a journey so important that he ought to subordinate all other concerns of life to it. Consider just a few of his resolutions:

- "Resolved, to endeavor to obtain for myself as much happiness, in the other world, as I possibly can."

- "Resolved, that I will live so as I shall wish I had done when I come to die."

- "Resolved, to endeavor to my utmost to act as I can think I should do, if I had already seen the happiness of heaven and hell's torments."

If the Holy Spirit is speaking to your heart as you read these words, why not make Edwards's resolutions your own? And why not start today?

Spiritual Insights on an Eternal Perspective

Many who have lived before me have brought tremendous blessing to me with their insights on the need to live with an eternal perspective. I think they might bless you as they have blessed me. Please allow these words to sink deep into your soul:

"God hath given to man a short time here upon earth, and yet upon this short time eternity depends" (Jeremy Taylor, 1613–1667, clergyman, Church of England).

"Time is short. Eternity is long. It is only reasonable that this short life be lived in the light of eternity" (Charles Spurgeon, 1834–1892, pastor, The Metropolitan Tabernacle, London).

"Lord, make me to know that I am so frail that I may die at any time—early morning, noon, night, midnight, cockcrow. I may die in any place. If I am in the house of sin, I may die there. If I am in the place of worship, I may die there. I may die in the street. I may die while undressing tonight. I may die in my sleep, die before I get to my work tomorrow morning. I may die in any occupation" (Charles Spurgeon).

"We are refugees from the sinking ship of this present world order, so soon to disappear; our hope is fixed in the eternal order, where the promises of God are made good to his people in perpetuity" (F.F. Bruce, 1910–1990, Bible scholar).

"Eternity to the godly is a day that has no sunset; eternity to the wicked is a night that has no sunrise" (Thomas Watson, 1620–1686, Puritan preacher, author).

"In our sad condition, our only consolation is the expectancy of another life. Here below all is incomprehensible" (Martin Luther, 1483–1546, professor of theology, reformer).

"Take courage. We walk in the wilderness today and in the Promised Land tomorrow" (Dwight L. Moody, 1837–1899, evangelist).

"However big and pressing the questions related to our present short life on earth may seem, they shrink into littleness compared with this timeless, measureless concern of death and the vast hereafter. How long earthly life looks to questing youth! How quickly fled it seems to the aged!" (J. Sidlow Baxter, 1903–1999, pastor, theologian).

"It ought to be the business of every day to prepare for our last day" (Matthew Henry, 1662–1714, Bible commentator, minister).

"This world is the land of the dying; the next is the land of the living" (Tryon Edwards, 1809–1894, theologian).

"Let thy hope of heaven master thy fear of death" (William Gurnall, 1617–1679, English author).

"Nothing is more contrary to a heavenly hope than an earthly heart" (William Gurnall).

"It is vanity to set your love on that which speedily passes away, and not to hasten to where everlasting joy abides" (Thomas à Kempis, 1380–1471, author, *The Imitation of Christ*).

"Our pleasant communion with our kind Christian friends is only broken off for a small moment, and is soon to be eternally resumed. These eyes of ours shall once more look upon their faces, and these ears of ours shall once more hear them speak…Blessed and happy indeed will that meeting be—better a thousand times than the parting! We parted in sorrow, and we shall meet in joy; we parted in stormy weather, and we shall meet in a calm harbor; we parted amidst pains and aches, and groans and infirmities; we shall meet with glorious bodies, able to serve our Lord forever without distraction" (J.C. Ryle, 1816–1900, Anglican bishop, Liverpool).

Lord, may we never forget these words!

The Big Ideas

- Bible prophecy can be a strong incentive to live with an eternal perspective.

- It is wise to perpetually ponder the realities of heaven in a diligent, active, and single-minded way. We ought to keep heaven at the forefront of our thoughts.

- Part of keeping an eternal perspective is a constant awareness of our mortality. Earthly life is just a dot in eternity.

- We each ought to resolve to live *now* in view of *then*.

Questions for Reflection

1. What steps can you take today to begin making an eternal perspective a central part of your thought processes?

2. What is the most meaningful thing you learned from this chapter?

Basic Bible Prophecy Quick Quiz

Wow! *We're done!* We have finished our task.

In the time we've spent together on Bible prophecy, we have explored the WHO, WHAT, WHEN, WHERE, and WHY of the end times. We have examined prophecy from these five different vantage points.

Before closing this book, I urge you to bring closure to your study of prophecy by perusing the quick quiz below. See how much you remember.

I suspect you will do quite well. Even if you don't, *no problem.* This book does not have to stay closed. You can review it as much as you feel necessary.

Primary Personalities of the End Times

Who are some of...

- the bad guys?
- the spiritual beings behind the scenes?
- the good guys?

Primary Events of the End Times

What are some of the events prophesied to take place...

- before the tribulation period?
- in the tribulation period?

- in the millennial kingdom?
- in the eternal state?

End-Times Geography

Can you summarize what you learned about…

- the centrality of Israel?
- the nations that will one day attack Israel?
- the revived Roman Empire?
- New Babylon?

God's Reasons for Giving Us End-Times Prophecy

How does prophecy motivate us to live…

- expectantly?
- righteously?
- with an eternal perspective?

Okay, that wasn't too bad, was it?

If you feel you've got a pretty good handle on most of these questions, then congratulations: *You now have a fundamental understanding of basic Bible prophecy.*

If you feel up to it, you can now "graduate" to more detailed books that can further enhance your understanding of Bible prophecy. To start you off, you might consider some other books I have written, all published by Harvest House Publishers:

- *The End Times in Chronological Order*
- *40 Days Through Revelation*
- *The Bible Prophecy Answer Book*

I pray that all my books are a blessing to you.

I look forward to seeing you at the rapture!

BIBLIOGRAPHY

Fruchtenbaum, Arnold. *The Footsteps of the Messiah*. San Antonio, TX: Ariel, 2004.

Hindson, Ed. *Revelation: Unlocking the Future*. Chattanooga, TN: AMG, 2002.

Hitchcock, Mark. *Bible Prophecy*. Wheaton, IL: Tyndale House, 1999.

Hoyt, Herman. *The End Times*. Chicago: Moody, 1969.

Ice, Thomas, and Timothy Demy. *When the Trumpet Sounds*. Eugene, OR: Harvest House, 1995.

LaHaye, Tim, and Ed Hindson, eds. *The Popular Bible Prophecy Commentary*. Eugene, OR: Harvest House, 2006.

———. *The Popular Encyclopedia of Bible Prophecy*. Eugene, OR: Harvest House, 2004.

Pentecost, J. Dwight. *Things to Come*. Grand Rapids, MI: Zondervan, 1964.

Rosenberg, Joel. *Epicenter*. Carol Stream, IL: Tyndale House, 2006.

Ryrie, Charles. *Basic Theology*. Wheaton, IL: Victor, 1986.

Showers, Renald. *Maranatha: Our Lord Come!* Bellmawr, NJ: The Friends of Israel Gospel Ministry, 1995.

Walvoord, John F. *End Times*. Nashville, TN: Word, 1998.

———. *The Prophecy Knowledge Handbook*. Wheaton, IL: Victor, 1990.

Walvoord, John F., and John E. Walvoord. *Armageddon, Oil, and the Middle East Crisis*. Grand Rapids: Zondervan, 1975.

NOTES

1. Robert P. Lightner, *Evangelical Theology* (Grand Rapids, MI: Baker Books, 1986), 57.

2. Charles C. Ryrie, *The Ryrie Study Bible* (Chicago: Moody), s.v. "Genesis 12:3."

3. David Cooper; cited in Arnold Fruchtenbaum, *The Footsteps of the Messiah* (San Antonio: Ariel Ministries, 2003), n.p.

4. Thomas Constable, "Dr. Constable's Expository Notes," 2010 edition, The Bible Study App, Olive Tree Software, 2020.

5. David L. Cooper, *The God of Israel* (Adelanto, CA: Biblical Research Society, 1973), iii.

6. Fruchtenbaum, *Footsteps of the Messiah*, n.p.

7. Ibid., 108.

8. Mark Hitchcock, *The End: A Complete Overview of Bible Prophecy and the End of Days* (Wheaton, IL: Tyndale House, 2012), 107.

9. J.C. Ryle, *Holiness* (Moscow, ID: Charles Nolan, 2001), xxiii.

10. Ibid., xv.

11. J.I. Packer, *Serving the People of God* (Great Britain: Paternoster Press, 1998), 23.

12. Ibid.

13. John F. Walvoord, "Revelation," in *The Bible Knowledge Commentary*, New Testament Edition, ed. John Walvoord and Roy Zuck (Colorado Springs: David C. Cook, 1983), n.p.

14. These include *The End Times in Chronological Order*, *The 8 Great Debates of Bible Prophecy*, *Jesus and the End Times*, *Bible Prophecy Answer Book*, *Israel on High Alert*, *End-Times Super Trends*, *Unmasking the Antichrist*, *New Babylon Rising*, *40 Days Through Daniel*, *40 Days Through Revelation*, and *Northern Storm Rising*.

15. David Reagan, "The Jews in Prophecy," Lamb and Lion Ministries, http://christianprophecy.org/articles/the-jews-in-prophecy/.

16. David Reagan, "The World's Hatred of Israel: Prophecy Fulfilled," Lamb and Lion Ministries, http://christianprophecy.org/articles/the-worlds-hatred-of-israel/.

17. I grant that 1 Peter 5:13 is debated among Bible scholars. Some suggest that Peter wrote from the literal city of Babylon along the Euphrates River. Others suggest that in this unique instance, "Babylon" might be a disguised metaphorical reference to Rome, intended to protect both Peter himself and the church in Rome from the Neronian persecution. John, however, based his references to Babylon in Revelation on the Old Testament alone, where *all* references to Babylon are literal.

18. John F. Walvoord, *End Times* (Nashville, TN: Word, 1998), 219.

19. J.I. Packer, ed., *Alive to God: Studies in Spirituality* (Downers Grove, IL: InterVarsity, 1992), 163.

20. Ibid., 171.

21. Richard Baxter, cited in Packer, 167.

22. Philip Yancey, *Where Is God When It Hurts?* (Grand Rapids, MI: Zondervan, 1977), 176.

23. John Wenham, *The Enigma of Evil: Can We Believe in the Goodness of God?* (Grand Rapids, MI: Zondervan, 1985), 55.

Bible Copyright Notifications